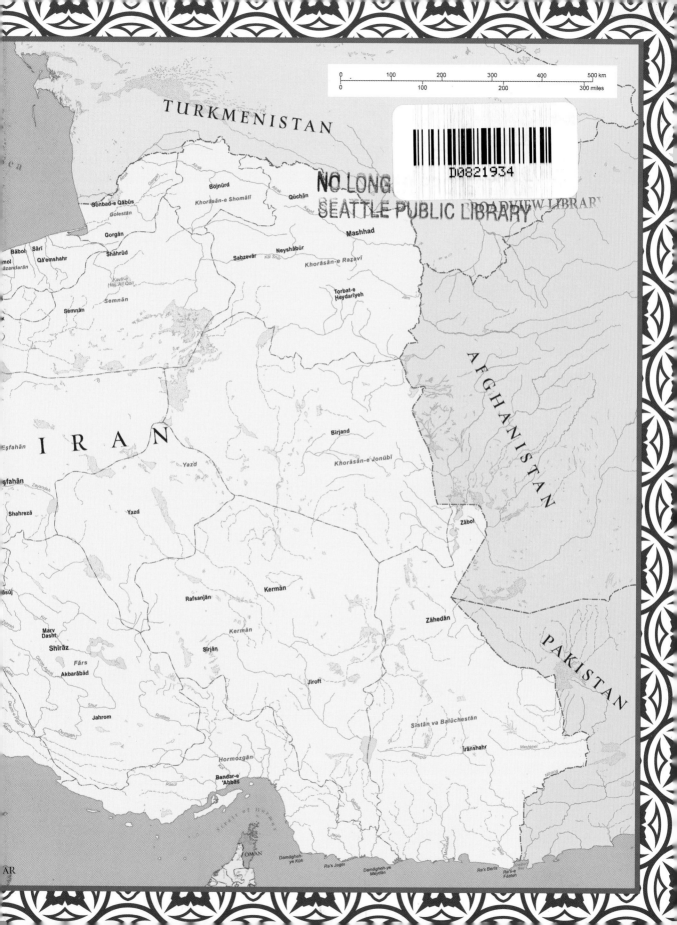

TURKMENISTAN

Qūchān

Bojnūrd

Khorāsān-e Shomālī

Gonbad-e Qābūs

Golestān

Mashhad

Gorgān

Bābol   Sārī

Qā'emshahr   Shāhrūd   Sabzevār   Neyshābūr

āzandarān   Kavīr-e   Khorāsān-e Razavī

Hajj 'Alī Qolī

Semnān   Semnān   Torbat-e
Heydarīyeh

AFGHANISTAN

IRAN

Eşfahān   Yazd   Bīrjand

şfahān   Zayandeh   Khorāsān-e Jonūbī

Shahrezā   Yazd   Zābol

āsūj   Rafsanjān   Kermān

Marv
Dasht   Kermān   Zāhedān

Shīrāz   PAKISTAN

Fārs   Sīrjān

Akbarābād   Jīroft

Jahrom   Sīstān va Balūchestān

Hormozgān   Īrānshahr

Bandar-e
'Abbās

Strait of Hormuz

OMAN   Damāgheh-
ye Kūh   Ra's Jagīn   Damāgheh-ye
Meydān   Ra's Berīs   Ra's-e
Fāsteh

ĀR

From the Land of
Nightingales & Roses

Maryam Sinaiee was born in Tehran, Iran, where she learned to cook from her mother, grandmothers, and aunts. She studied ancient Iranian languages at Tehran University and has contributed several articles on pre-Islamic Persian culture and religion to Iranian publications. In 2011, Maryam moved to the UK, where she decided to follow her life-long passion for food and food writing. Leaving behind her career as a foreign correspondent and political analyst, she set up her food blog, The Persian Fusion, which is now one of the most popular Persian food blogs in English. *From the Land of Nightingales and Roses* is her first cookbook.

thepersianfusion.com
@sinaiee_maryam

From the Land of
Nightingales
& Roses

Recipes from the Persian Kitchen

Maryam Sinaiee

Interlink Books

An imprint of Interlink Publishing Group, Inc.
Northampton, Massachusetts

First published in 2019 by

INTERLINK BOOKS
An imprint of Interlink Publishing Group, Inc.
46 Crosby Street, Northampton, MA 01060
www.interlinkbooks.com

Library of Congress Cataloging-in-Publication Data available
ISBN 978-1-62371-967-8

1 3 5 7 9 10 8 6 4 2

Design by Jessie Price
Photography and styling by Maryam Sinaiee
Cover photograph by Jessica Griffiths

Printed in China by 1010 Printing International Ltd

To request our 48-page, full-color catalog, please call us toll free at
1-800-238-LINK, visit our website at www.interlinkbooks.com, or
send us an e-mail at: info@interlinkbooks.com.

To my mom, grandmas, and aunties, who were always a source of inspiration and taught me to cook.

Introduction

My love affair with cooking goes back a long way, to my childhood, to the kitchens of my extended family, and to the stunning dishes the women in my family prepared on a daily basis. I was born in Tehran into a family from Tabriz, a city in northwest Iran famous for its highly refined cuisine. My father's side of the family had moved to the capital decades before I was born and my mother's side did so when I was still quite young, but both families always closely guarded their traditions, including anything to do with food. When my mother was young, women were expected to excel in the art of cooking, and so my mother, grandmothers, and aunts were all fabulous cooks.

My father was a colonel in the army so we moved around quite a lot. When I was thirteen or fourteen, we moved to a town in northeast Iran, and into a house surrounded by apricot and almond trees big enough to climb up and hide in. Pink rose bushes lined the paths between the trees, and in the late spring and early summer the scent of the roses filled the air. Nightingales nesting in the bushes would sing out at the top of their lungs each morning as the sun rose in the sky. The nightingales were so tiny, and I always wondered how these birds could produce such loud, beautiful notes for hours and hours.

When my grandma and aunt came to visit, the roses found a culinary use: they decided to make rosewater. I don't know where or how they found a proper copper distilling pot, but the next thing we knew they had set one up in a building next to the house. For the next few days, they would get up at sunrise to fill large sheets with the fragrant roses that had bloomed overnight. The petals from these were gradually fed into the copper pot and mixed with water to produce bottle after bottle of rosewater—enough to send to all the neighbors. The title of this book refers to an affectionate term locals have for Iran: the land of nightingales and roses, because we are—or, rather, used to be—obsessed with romance and poetry. For me, this phrase also perfectly encapsulates our cuisine: beautifully, almost magically, flavored, yet always rooted in nature.

I always loved to hang out near the kitchen as a child, to watch as my grandmother made huge meatballs and stuffed them with whole boiled eggs, walnuts, and dried golden plums, or to hover at my mom's arm as she fried her carefully shaped kotlet (ground meat fritters), hoping for a bite of the first one out of the pan. These fabulous women would spend days making their gorgeous jams and pickles with the seasonal fruits and vegetables on hand, jars of which would then adorn the shelves throughout the year, creating a rainbow of color. Together, they painstakingly baked sweets of all kinds and piled them onto silver platters

to celebrate the New Year and other festivities. All this I watched in amazement, quietly absorbing their extraordinary knowledge of ingredients, spices, and herbs.

The food served in our family was always beautifully presented. Nothing was taken to the table before being meticulously garnished with saffron, yogurt, nuts, crispy caramelized onions, or herbs so that every dish looked like a work of art. From an early age I learned that food must not only please the nose and the palate but also the eye, and I grew up with the belief that cooking was an artistic expression, not a chore.

The first time I prepared a meal I was about nine or ten. My parents were out, and I knew they would be returning around noon with some friends. So, I did what my mom would have done, and made a plan for lunch. It was simple—some rice, a salad, and an egg dish—but with the help of a servant I set out a beautiful spread with bowls of my mom's pickles and preserves and whatever else I could find in our pantry. My parents were very surprised and proud when they saw the feast, but it wasn't until years later that I began to cook regularly. In the meantime, I just kept watching, learning and, of course, eating.

Though I loved cooking and dreamed of being a chef, like most Iranian parents in the 1970s, mine wanted me to study medicine or engineering. Then the revolution in 1979 drastically changed the course of our lives —my father was forced to leave his job and the new regime closed all the universities, leading to a hiatus in my studies. When they reopened three years later, I decided to study ancient Persian languages and culture, but I never gave up my love for food. I studied Persian and other cuisines in the same way I studied ancient texts for my degree. During this time I married into a family of serious foodies who I learned even more from. Years passed, and I fell in love again, this time with politics, and eventually entered the world of journalism. But I kept dreaming about writing my very own cookbook one day.

In 2011, following the controversial presidential elections of 2009, the political circumstances in my country forced my family and I to escape Iran, aware we could probably never go back. As we settled in our new life in Britain, I soon realized that the delicious home cooking I had been brought up on was missing from the repertoires of even the most adventurous cooks I met. Many assumed that Persian food was too daunting to prepare at home, or needed too many ingredients that are hard to find, but gadgets such as the food processor, and an array of good-quality ingredients now available from speciality stores, ethnic food stores, and even supermarkets make cooking Persian dishes outside Iran much easier today than it once was. I wanted people to see how incredibly rich and diverse our cuisine really is and so I began dreaming about a Persian cookbook again, and this time I put everything in writing. As I frantically cooked my way through the old and familiar recipes from my childhood, as well as the new dishes I'd discovered more recently on

travels in Iran, I found a way to connect my past and present lives. In 2015, I began writing a food blog, The Persian Fusion, which led, eventually, to this book you now hold in your hands. This is the book I have dreamed of writing since I was a little girl. I hope you enjoy cooking—and eating—the recipes it contains.

Persian Cuisine

What we call Persian cuisine, or Iranian cuisine if you like, is the result of a very long historical process. Since antiquity, the country called Persia by the classic historians, and Iran by its own people, has expanded to include new far-away lands and then shrunk back again many times over. This has hugely enriched the food culture with diverse ingredients and cooking methods. The country's unique position in the middle of the Silk Road also had a big role in the development of the Persian cuisine. The Persian Empire no longer exists, but its direct descendant, Iran, is still a vast country with climates ranging from very cold and dry to subtropical, so there is a huge variety of ingredients available for cooking. Today Iran is home to several distinct ethnic groups speaking different languages and boasts a very sophisticated cuisine with considerable variations defined by culture, geography, and climate.

Classic Persian dishes are usually sour (torsh), sweet (shīrīn), or sweet and sour (malas). Traditional dishes are rarely hot and spicy (tond), but in southern regions cooking is highly influenced by Indian, Arab, and even African cuisines and so spicy food is more usual. Subtle spicing is a very key element of classic Persian cooking. With few exceptions, spices are there to contribute to the taste and smell but not to dominate. I believe smell is the most defining characteristic of Persian dishes, which are so often perfumed with our beloved saffron or rosewater as well as sweet-smelling spices such as cinnamon, Persian caraway (zīreh), rose petals, and cardamom.

Meat typically has the same standing in a dish as vegetables, nuts, and fruits. We eat a huge range of vegetables and fruits, and often name our dishes after the vegetable they are cooked with, not whatever kind of meat that's used in them. Lamb and chicken feature in traditional dishes and beef is now widely used, though in the old days cattle were only raised for meat in the Caspian Sea regions. Classic fish dishes mainly come from the northern Caspian Sea region and the southern provinces on the shores of the Persian Gulf. These two regions are more than 1,250 miles (2,000 kilometers) apart with tall mountain ranges, huge plains, and deserts lying between them. Traditionally, the people living inland rarely ate any fish, and the use of seafood is limited in Persian dishes, since Islam, like Judaism, prohibits eating non-scaly fish and shellfish. For the same reason the majority of Iranians don't eat pork. Selling pork is banned by Islamic laws, but Armenians and other Christian groups raise pigs for their own consumption.

The Seasons

Seasons and seasonality are at the very center of Persian life. We hugely value the first fruit, vegetables, or herbs that appear with each season, which we call "nōbarāneh" meaning "first of the harvest" or "new produce." Nōbarāneh are given as gifts to friends and relatives, though often only in tiny amounts, since they can be really expensive even if they're as ordinary as green plums or apricots. We take a lot of pleasure in eating the first of the green baby almonds or succulent stalks of rhubarb in spring and when these crops become more available and affordable, we incorporate them into our everyday dishes.

The Persian calendar, unlike the western calendar, is based around the cycle of nature. Our year begins in March with Nōrūz (new day), which is the day of the spring equinox. Accordingly, summer begins with the summer solstice; fall with the fall equinox; and winter with the winter solstice. Although the climate varies hugely from region to region, the four seasons remain quite distinct. Early spring is warm enough to picnic in green fields or orchards painted white and pink with almond, plum, cherry, and apricot blossoms. Melting snow from the high mountain peaks fill the rivers and streams and wild plants abound. As the hot, dry summer approaches, the grasses and wild flowers wither and die and everyone begins praying for rain. People flock to the Caspian Sea or the mountains to enjoy the cooler air. Outdoor eating takes center stage with barbecues, fresh salads, and plenty of pickles. Autumn arrives with colorful leaves, abundant produce, and the rain everybody has been waiting for. Unsurprisingly, Iranians find these rare cloudy, rainy days highly romantic. Fall is the time to make jars and jars of pickles, jams, and relishes to help us through the coldest months. In many regions, winters can be harsh with lots of snow and ice forcing people to stay indoors—but never alone. Friends and family gather to spend the long, dark evenings together, sharing food and enjoying endless cups of tea with little sweetmeats.

Our calendar is punctuated by several festivals closely tied in with the seasons—like Nōrūz in spring. These have been celebrated since ancient times despite the Islamification of the country 1,400 years ago, and form an integral part of Iranian—or Persian—identity. In early summer we celebrate Tīrgān, a festival associated with rain to ward off drought in the hottest months. In agricultural communities, fall begins with harvest festivals, which take place soon after the fall equinox, then as the days grow shorter and colder, Iranians celebrate Yaldā on the eve of the winter solstice.

Because our lives—and our stomachs—are led by the seasons, it made perfect sense for me to organize the recipes in this book into seasonal chapters. This structure enables me to draw a picture not only of Persian food, but also of Persian life. Each recipe in this book appears in the chapter most suited to it—to the

seasonal availability of its key ingredients, to how hearty and filling it is to eat, and to how and when it is traditionally made and enjoyed in Iran. Of course, if you wish to make a spring dish in autumn, I am not going to stand in your way.

"Hot" and "Cold" Food

A unique feature of Persian cuisine is the stress on balancing the ingredients in a dish according to an elaborate medical tradition known as teb-be sonnati, based on the teachings of Galen and Hippocrates. This teaches that food must not only please the eye, palate, and nose, but also benefit the body by maintaining, or even restoring, its natural balance. According to this system, ingredients are divided into two main categories: "hot" and "cold." This has no relevance to spiciness or the temperature of the food. High-energy, high-protein ingredients such as most meats, honey, dates, nuts, and some herbs like mint, summer savory, and dill are considered "hot," while many vegetables and fruit, especially the sour ones, are "cold." The "hot" and "cold" must be balanced in each meal in order to maintain good health. This balance is best demonstrated in fesenjūn, a stew of duck, chicken, or lamb meatballs with a thick sauce made from ground walnuts and pomegranate paste. Walnuts are "hot" so they are balanced with pomegranate, which is "cold."

Belief in the merits of this system is so deep that most Iranians will shudder at the thought of pairing fish with yogurt, or eating watermelons after a dish made with zucchini, since all of these are considered to be very "cold" and too much "cold" food is believed to cause digestive problems and lead to low energy levels. On the other hand, too much "hot" food can cause skin rashes and hot flashes. When a "cold" dish is served, a "hot" dessert such as one made with dates will follow to maintain the balance. But that's not all: food must be taken in accordance with each individual's temperament. "Cold" food is better for individuals with a "hot" temperament and vice versa. The system is much more complicated than the simple account I've given, but even having a general idea might be helpful in understanding the nature of our cuisine and why we do not combine certain ingredients in a dish.

Hospitality and Food Etiquette

Iranian hospitality demands that guests be offered a hot or cold beverage as soon as they arrive. In summer this is usually an iced diluted fruit syrup (sharbat) or fruit juice to ward off the heat; in the colder months it's tea or coffee. Seasonal fruits, cookies, pastries, and roasted nuts are offered to guests both before and after dinner. We often entertain in large numbers at home so the food is served buffet-style or around the sofreh (a cloth spread on the floor around which people sit to eat). In more traditional communities, men and women may be served in separate rooms

and the eldest or most senior person in the room is always offered a place at the top of the room, i.e. as far from the door as possible.

It must be hard for those unfamiliar with Persian culture to know how to respond when total strangers offer them food, insist on taking them home to share a meal, or refuse to take money for a commodity or service. There is a very elaborate etiquette involved in all these behaviors. For example, you must always offer food or drinks to those around you before eating anything yourself. In traditional communities the person offered food is supposed to refuse the first time, then refuse it again when it's repeated, only accepting the third time it is offered. I'm quite useless with this custom (called ta'arof) and won't engage in it unless I absolutely must in order to avoid offending people. Like many old customs ta'arof is gradually dying out, probably because people can't function in today's modern world with the many complications arising from it.

Structure of Meals

Our meals aren't divided into courses. A typical Persian meal will often start with a hearty soup (āsh), or a yogurt-based chilled soup (ābdūgh) when the weather is hot. Soups are our only real appetizers. The main dish or dishes—there is often more than one—are served alongside an array of smaller dishes, pickles, fresh herbs, salads, and bread. These are called "mokhallaffāt," meaning "other, less important stuff" or "sundries." Some restaurants now serve mokhallaffāt separately as appetizers, but the traditional way is to scatter these around the table or sofreh in small bowls or plates.

We are not big dessert eaters, and will usually just have fresh fruit after a meal, but in the colder months fruit jams, saffron-perfumed rice pudding, and halvā may be offered. Food is often followed by endless cups of tea and small confections, pastries and candies, dates, or other sweet dried fruit such as dried white mulberries for people to pick at as they talk and digest.

Recipes in this Book

I've cherry-picked my recipes from the classic cuisine as well as the regional cuisines of Gilan, Mazandaran, Azarbaijan, Kurdistan, Hormozgan, and Khuzestan, to name a few, and I have made every effort to make the recipes as simple as possible. Some of these dishes are only made on festive occasions in Iran and are a bit tricky, but these are balanced out with plenty that are quick and easy to make, as well as being a joy to eat. I have added my own personal touch throughout—a little less of this, a little more of that, or an ingredient or spice I feel will make the food more delicious, but nothing I have done will make the dish unrecognizable from its original incarnation.

All the cooking times should be taken as guides, since not all ovens and stovetop burners behave in the same way. You know your oven best, so please allow for adjustments.

A Note on Persian Words

The Persian language Farsi is written in Arabic script in which most vowels are not represented in writing. The Latinisation of Persian words is quite difficult since there are many methods. I've chosen a simple phonetic representation to make the pronunciation of food names easier but have left geographical names as they are. Some dishes have more than one name or different names in various languages or dialects. I will provide the most common of these names with the phonetic alphabet.

Only some vowels and a few consonants are pronounced very differently from English. Below is a key to the pronunciation of vowels and consonants not occurring in English.

Symbol	Pronunciation	Example
ā	ah as aa in naan	āsh (soup)
a	a as in lad	barbarī (a type of bread)
e	e as in bed	bādemjān (eggplant)
eh	long e at the end of a word	līteh (a kind of pickle)
ī	ee as in see	sīr (garlic)
o	o as in orchid	morgh (chicken)
ō	similar to ow in window	polō (pilaw)
ū	u as in goose	kūfteh (meatball)
gh	similar to g	ghormeh sabzī (a type of stew)
kh	similar to k	khormā (dates)

SPRING

The first day of spring marks the Persian new year and is, undoubtedly, the most important calendar event in the lives of Iranians. Nōrūz, meaning "new day," is celebrated from the exact moment of the vernal equinox, which has been calculated by astronomers since ancient times and can fall in the morning or even in the middle of the night. Everyone gathers around a special table or sofreh (a cloth spread on the floor) waiting for the radio announcement that the year has turned. Right after the announcement, we eat something sweet to encourage a sweet life in the days ahead.

The Nōrūz spread, known as haftsīn, is dressed with candles and mirrors symbolizing light; grains and fruits symbolizing plenty; painted eggs to symbolize fertility; sprouted wheat or other seeds to symbolize the rejuvenation of nature; goldfish in a bowl of water to symbolize life; and vinegar—or wine for those unscrupulous about religious prohibitions—to symbolize age and wisdom.

The spread is decorated with narcissus, tulips, and hyacinths, the first spring flowers to bloom. Most people will put a copy of the Quran or their holy book in their haftsīn; many others will have a copy of Dīvān-e Hāfez, a collection of poems by Hāfez, who lived in the fourteenth century and is probably our most revered poet. His poems exalt love, wine, and beauty and condemn religious hypocrisy.

On the thirteenth day of the new year, Sīzdeh be Dar is celebrated by taking to the woods, mountains, and parks for a day-long picnic to cast off evil. This holiday brings the Nōrūz festivities to an end.

We start the spring with special foods prepared for the new year: this is the season to enjoy spring lamb, fresh herbs, and sweet vegetables. In this chapter you will find some of the best foods that we enjoy during the new year holidays, comforting yet light spring dishes, and plenty of foods that can be easily packed up for picnics in the countryside or parks—a favorite Iranian pastime.

Spring recipes

Eshkaneh-ye Rīvās
Rhubarb, Onion, and Egg Soup

According to Iranian mythology, Mashya and Mashyānag, the first human couple, emerged from a rhubarb plant and filled the world with their offspring to assist the forces of Light in their relentless battle against Darkness. Come spring, wild rhubarb spreads its leaves all over the Iranian plains and mountains as it has for thousands of years. This rustic soup is from eastern Iran, where wild rhubarb is plentiful. Locals build up the soil around the stalks to produce very tender pinkish cream or pale green stalks similar to forced pink rhubarb—both are perfect for this soup.

SERVES 4

3 tablespoons (1½ oz/40 g) butter
2 medium onions, thinly sliced
1 tablespoon dried mint
½ teaspoon ground turmeric
1½ tablespoons flour
4 cups (1 liter) boiling water
3 stalks of rhubarb
Salt and black pepper, to taste
4 small eggs
Pinch of sugar (optional)
Mint sprigs, to garnish
Dried flatbread such as lavāsh, to serve

Melt the butter in a saucepan over medium-low heat and cook the onions until golden but not brown, stirring often so they are evenly colored. Sprinkle on the mint, turmeric, and flour and cook for 2 minutes. Add the water and bring to a boil. Lower the heat, cover, and cook gently for 10–15 minutes.

Slice the rhubarb into small chunks. Add to the saucepan and stir well. Season with salt and plenty of black pepper and simmer gently for 5 minutes with the lid on.

Break one egg into a cup and gently slide it into the soup. Repeat with the rest of the eggs. Simmer for 10 minutes until the eggs are cooked through. Taste and add a pinch of sugar if the soup is too sour.

Place an egg in each serving bowl and ladle the soup over it. Garnish with some mint and serve with dried flatbread broken into pieces to soak in the soup.

Āsh Reshteh
Noodle, Legume, and Herb Soup

This soup is often made on the eve of the new year to bring good luck. The word for noodles (reshteh) also means string, and eating noodles at the start of the year is said to help to untangle the strings of life. Āsh reshteh is also traditionally made the day after a loved one has departed on a journey. In this case, the long noodles symbolize invisible threads that will help the traveler find their way home. Eggless linguini or udon noodles work as a substitute for the Persian soup noodles, but it's a good idea to thicken the soup with a little flour, since Persian noodles are tossed in flour before drying.

SERVES 6

¼ cup (60 ml) oil

3 onions, finely sliced

2 teaspoons ground turmeric

8 cups (2 liters) boiling water or beef stock

10 cups (10½ oz/300 g) spinach, coarsely chopped

⅔ cup (1½ oz/40 g) cilantro, coarsely chopped

⅔ cup (1½ oz/40 g) flat-leaf parsley, coarsely chopped

⅔ cup (1½ oz/40 g) coarsely chopped chives

1 cup (3½ oz/100 g) Persian soup noodles, broken into pieces

1 x 15 oz (425 g) can chickpeas, drained

1 x 15 oz (425 g) can borlotti beans, drained

½ x 15 oz (425 g) can green lentils, drained

Sea salt and black pepper

1 tablespoon flour (optional)

1 quantity fried mint (page 276)

1 quantity fried garlic (page 276)

Liquid kashk or white wine vinegar, to serve

Heat the oil in a Dutch oven or deep saucepan over medium heat and fry the onions until golden brown. Add the turmeric and swirl around for 1–2 minutes. Remove a couple of tablespoons of the onions for garnishing the soup if you wish.

Pour in the boiling water and bring back to a boil. Add the spinach and herbs. Cover and simmer gently for 45 minutes.

Add the noodles, chickpeas, beans, and lentils and cook until the noodles have softened. If the soup is too thin, add a little flour dissolved in water to thicken it (about 1 tablespoon should be enough). Taste and add salt and black pepper, if necessary, and simmer gently for 10 minutes. This soup should be quite thick.

Ladle the soup into bowls and garnish with the fried mint, fried garlic, and reserved onions. Offer kashk (a yogurt-based product with a strong cheesy flavor) or vinegar at the table.

Māhī Shekam Por
Northern-Style Stuffed Fish

This is a luxurious dish enjoyed in the regions surrounding the Caspian Sea. In the old days, before people had ovens in their homes, fish was sent to the local bakery to be baked after the bread-baking was done. When made at home, the fish was steamed over twigs or pebbles in a clay dish with a domed lid similar to a tagine, called gamej in Gilan Province. The fish traditionally used for this dish is Caspian kutum, which has very white, tender, sweet flesh, but the stuffing also works brilliantly with trout. On special occasions, I stuff a whole salmon, which makes for a spectacular centerpiece

SERVES 4

1 large or 2 medium-sized trout, cleaned and descaled

1 teaspoon salt

5 tablespoons oil

2 onions, finely chopped

¼ teaspoon ground turmeric

3 cloves of garlic, finely chopped

⅔ cup (1½ oz/40 g) cilantro, chopped

⅓ cup (¾ oz/20 g) mint, chopped

⅔ cup (2½ oz/70 g) walnuts, chopped

Seeds from one pomegranate

½ teaspoon cinnamon

½ teaspoon ground black pepper

¼ cup (60 ml) pomegranate molasses

A few sprigs of mint, to garnish

Preheat the oven to 350°F (180°C). Rinse the fish to remove any remaining scales and dry with paper towels. Sprinkle half the salt over the skin and inside the belly and rub it in.

Heat 2 tablespoons of the oil in a frying pan and cook the onions until golden. Add the turmeric and garlic and cook for 2 minutes. Remove from the heat and combine with the chopped herbs, walnuts, pomegranate seeds (reserving some to garnish), cinnamon, the remaining salt, black pepper, and pomegranate molasses. Stuff the fish with the walnut mixture and tie with kitchen twine to secure it.

Line a baking dish with parchment paper and place the fish in the dish. Drizzle with the remaining oil and bake, uncovered, for 50 minutes to 1 hour, or until the skin is golden (for smaller fish, reduce the cooking time by around 15 minutes). Garnish with pomegranate seeds and mint sprigs and serve immediately with kateh (page 239).

Sabzī Polō bā Māhī
Herbed Rice with Pan-Fried Fish

On the eve of Nōrūz many families cook this rice dish and serve it with pan-fried fish and a herby frittata (kūkū sabzī, page 29). In Iran, the green of the rice is associated with the rejuvenation of nature and the fish symbolizes life, making this the perfect meal to welcome in spring.

SERVES 4-6

FOR THE RICE

⅔ cup (1½ oz/40 g) cilantro, finely chopped

⅓ cup (¾ oz/20 g) flat-leaf parsley, finely chopped

⅔ cup (1½ oz/40 g) finely chopped chives

⅔ cup (1½ oz/40 g) dill, finely chopped

2 sprigs of fenugreek greens, finely chopped (optional)

2 cups (14 oz/400 g) white long grain rice

3 stalks of green garlic or 3 cloves of garlic, finely chopped

2 tablespoons oil

2 potatoes, thickly sliced

Sea salt

2 tablespoons (1 oz/30 g) butter, melted with 1 tablespoon water

½ teaspoon saffron water (page 278)

FOR THE PAN-FRIED FISH

⅔ cup (3 oz/80 g) all-purpose flour

1 teaspoon ground turmeric

1 teaspoon salt

½ teaspoon ground black pepper

4 sea bass fillets, scaled

⅓ cup (80 ml) oil

1½ tablespoons (¾ oz/20 g) butter

Lime wedges and radishes, to serve

Mix the chopped herbs together. Prepare and boil the rice according to the instructions for chelō (page 236). As soon as the grains begin to float to the surface, add one-quarter of the herbs. Combine the rest with the garlic and set aside. Once the rice is soft but still has a firm bite in the center, drain it in a colander.

Heat the oil in a large pot until very hot. Remove from the heat and arrange the sliced potatoes in the pan in one layer, then sprinkle with salt. Gently pile one-third of the rice in the center in a mound. Sprinkle the rice with one-third of the herb and garlic mixture, and repeat until all the rice and herbs are used up. Wrap the lid in a clean dish towel and cover the pot tightly.

Return the pot to medium heat and cook for a few minutes until the side of the pot sizzles when touched with a wet finger. Pour the melted butter over the rice, then replace the dish towel and the lid. Steam over very low heat for 30 minutes, then test the rice by gently tapping the top of the mound; the rice will "tremble" if it's done.

Just before serving, transfer some of the rice to a small bowl. Add the saffron water and mix gently. Place the rest of the rice on a platter and cover with the saffron rice. Lift the crisp potato pieces (tahdīg) from the bottom of the pot and arrange around the rice.

For the pan-fried fish, mix the flour, turmeric, salt, and pepper in a shallow dish. Coat the fish fillets in the flour mixture on both sides. Shake to remove any excess.

Heat the oil and butter in a frying pan over medium heat until very hot and add the fish, flesh side down. Cook until golden, about 4 minutes, then flip over and cook on the skin side until tender, 3–4 minutes. Drain on paper towels and serve with the rice, potatoes, radishes, and lime wedges.

Rān-e Beryān
Stuffed Leg of Lamb with Yogurt and Saffron

This recipe stems from one I found in the sixteenth-century Persian cookbook, *Treatise on the Art of Cooking,* where a whole lamb is stuffed with fruits and spices and baked in a tanūr (clay oven). As it would be hard to fit a whole lamb in a domestic oven, I have opted here for a butterflied leg instead. My mom used to coat big chunks of cooked lamb with yogurt and saffron and then bake it in the oven. I have adopted this technique here: the yogurt keeps the meat moist and creates a delicious golden crust.

SERVES 8–10

1 butterflied leg of lamb (about 4½ lb/2 kg)

Salt and pepper

1 tablespoon oil

1 onion, quartered

4 cloves of garlic

2 bay leaves

1 tablespoon whole black peppercorns

1 tablespoon barberries, to garnish (optional)

scant ½ cup (4¼ oz/120 g) Greek yogurt

¼ teaspoon ground saffron

FOR THE STUFFING

2 tablespoons (1 oz/30 g) butter

2 onions, finely chopped

12 prunes, pitted

¼ cup (1 oz/30 g) barberries, rinsed

½ cup (1¾ oz/50 g) walnuts, coarsely chopped

1 heaped tablespoon dried rose petals, lightly crushed

¼ teaspoon cinnamon

½ teaspoon ground cumin

½ teaspoon ground black pepper

¼ teaspoon salt

To make the stuffing, melt the butter in a large Dutch oven and cook the onions until golden brown. Transfer to a bowl and mix with the other stuffing ingredients.

Place the butterflied leg on a chopping board, skin side down. Make incisions in the thickest parts of the meat to help spread it out evenly but be careful not to cut all the way through. Rub with salt and pepper. Spread the stuffing over the meat, keeping about 1 inch (2½ cm) free at the edges. Roll up and tie securely with twine, making sure the stuffing is completely enclosed.

Heat the oil in your Dutch oven and brown the meat on all sides. Turn it seam side down and add the onion, garlic, bay leaves, and peppercorns. Pour in enough boiling water to come one-third of the way up the meat. Bring to a boil and skim off any scum. Lower the heat to a gentle simmer, cover the pot, and braise for at least 2½ hours. You may need to top up the water now and then to stop it drying out. Remove the meat and set aside.

Take 2 tablespoons of the fat from the surface of the broth and set aside. Boil the remaining broth until it has reduced to about 1 cup (250 ml). Pass through a sieve and keep warm.

Fry the barberries in a little oil for a minute or until they are shiny and puffed up. Preheat the broiler. Mix the yogurt with the saffron and a pinch of salt. Remove the twine from the meat and return to the pot, along with the reserved fat. Coat the top and sides of the meat with the yogurt. Broil for 20–25 minutes or until golden brown. Garnish with the barberries and serve with reshteh polō (page 205) and the reduced broth.

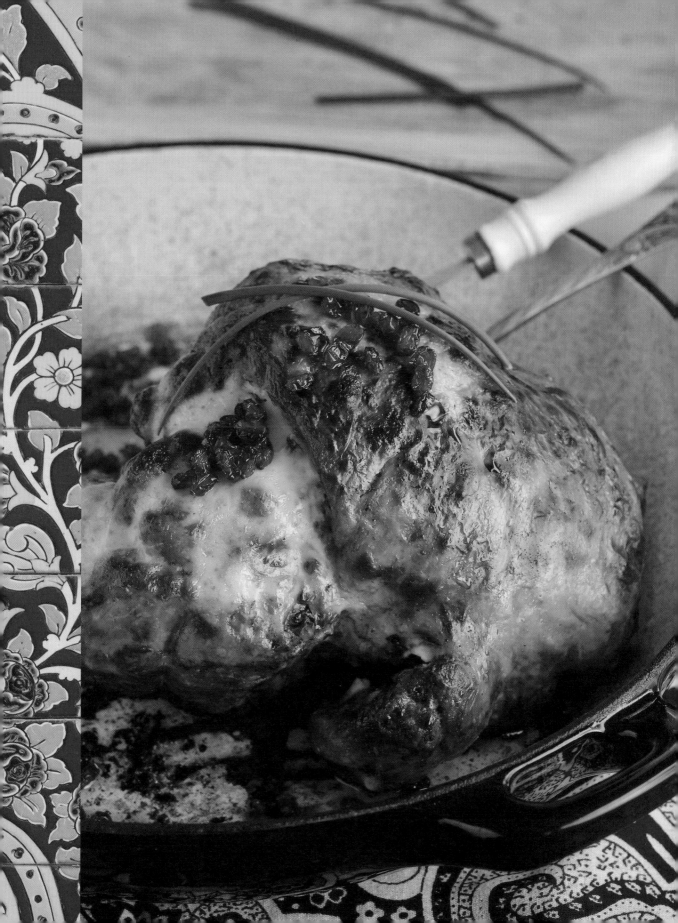

Khoresht-e Rīvas
Lamb and Rhubarb Stew

I first had this dish at a school-friend's house. I had never tasted anything like it before—herby and sharp with meltingly tender chunks of lamb. I asked my friend's mother for the recipe then raced home to tell my own mom about it. At my house, we only ever ate rhubarb raw with a pinch of salt. Needless to say, khoresht-e rīvas quickly became a family favorite. Several other spring stews are made with this base of lamb, mint, and parsley, but it's not easy to find their star ingredient (young wild artichoke stalks, baby green almonds, or sour green plums) outside of Iran. This will improve greatly by sitting for a day or two. If you make this in advance, add the rhubarb just before serving.

SERVES 4-6

5 tablespoons oil

2 onions, finely chopped

14 oz (400 g) boneless lamb neck or lean shoulder, cut into large chunks

½ teaspoon ground turmeric

½ teaspoon salt

¼ teaspoon ground black pepper

2 cups (4¼ oz/120 g) flat-leaf parsley, finely chopped

¾ cup (1¾ oz/50 g) mint, finely chopped

1 tablespoon flour

4 large stalks of rhubarb, cut into 1 inch (2½ cm) pieces

Sugar, to taste

Heat 2 tablespoons of the oil in a Dutch oven and lightly brown the onions. Add the lamb, turmeric, salt, and pepper and fry until the meat is lightly browned on all sides. Pour over enough boiling water to cover by an inch or so. Cover the pot, bring to a boil, then lower the heat to a gentle simmer and braise for 1½ hours, or until the lamb is tender.

Heat the remaining 3 tablespoons oil in a frying pan and sauté the chopped herbs for 4–5 minutes until they darken in color. Sprinkle over the flour and cook for 3 minutes, stirring constantly. Add the herbs to the lamb and simmer for an additonal 30 minutes or until the minty sauce has the consistency of very thick gravy.

Add the rhubarb and stir through. Cook, covered, on medium-low heat until the rhubarb is soft, around 10 minutes. Don't stir, or you will break up the delicate pieces. Taste, and add a pinch of sugar if the sauce is too sour. Serve with chelō (page 236) or kateh (page 239).

Ābgūsht-e Sabzī
Lamb and Bean Hotpot

In his book about Persia, Jakob Eduard Polak, the nineteenth-century Austrian physician and advisor to the Shah of Iran, listed fourteen different types of ābgūsht made in the court kitchens. Ābgūsht-e sabzī is a traditional hotpot perfumed with tarragon, mint, and chives or whatever aromatic wild herbs are available. Like most ābgūshts, this spring delight is served in three parts: as a broth, a rich meat stew, and a pâté-like mash (gūsht kūbīdeh) that tastes great both warm and cold.

SERVES 4–6

2 tablespoons oil

2 onions, finely chopped

1¾ lb (800 g) lamb shoulder on the bone, cut into large chunks

1½ teaspoons ground turmeric

3 cloves of garlic

1 small cinnamon stick

3 dried limes, pricked with a knife (optional)

2 x 15 oz (425 g) cans cannellini or butter beans

1½ teaspoons sea salt flakes

¼ teaspoon ground white pepper (black is fine too)

½ cup (1 oz/30 g) tarragon, finely chopped

½ cup (1 oz/30 g) mint, finely chopped

½ cup (1 oz/30 g) chives, finely chopped

2 potatoes, peeled and cut into large cunks

Small pinch of saffron threads

Flatbread, to serve

Heat the oil in a large Dutch oven and soften the onions over medium heat. Add the meat and the turmeric and fry until the meat is lightly browned on all sides. Add the garlic, cinnamon, and enough boiling water to cover the meat. Drop in the dried limes, if using, and bring to a boil. Lower the heat to a gentle simmer, cover, and braise for 2 hours or until the lamb is tender.

Drain and rinse the beans and add them to the pot with the salt and white pepper. Top up with a little boiling water if needed: you will need about 1 cup (250 ml) of broth per person to serve as the soup. Add the chopped herbs and stir, then arrange the potatoes on top of the meat. Cover tightly and simmer for 20 minutes or until the potatoes are soft.

Add salt and pepper to taste. Sprinkle the saffron over and simmer for a further 10 minutes. Using a slotted spoon, carefully transfer the meat, beans, and potatoes to a bowl. Discard the cinnamon stick and keep the broth warm over low heat.

Place half of the meat, bean, and potato mixture in a serving dish along with the dried limes. Cover and keep warm in a low oven. Mash the rest into a rough pâté-like paste. Add a little of the broth if it's too thick, then spread on a plate. Make indentations on the surface and pour over a tablespoon or two of the broth.

Ladle the broth into bowls and let everyone soak as much bread in it as they wish. Then serve the meat stew and the pâté with more bread and plenty of relishes and condiments, such as torshī mashhadī (page 264), sabzī khordan (page 98) and sliced white radishes (torob) sprinkled with salt and lemon juice.

Kotlet

Beef and Potato Fritters

Our food on Sīzdeh be Dar—a day of picnicking that marks the end of our New Year festivities—always included a big batch of these fritters, along with a savory cake like kūkū sabzī (page 29) or kūkū-ye lūbiyā (page 93). These dishes can be prepared ahead, they're easy to pack, and I have yet to meet anyone who doesn't love them. We would eat them rolled into flatbread with my mom's crunchy vegetable pickles (shūr, page 273), radishes, and fresh herbs. The fritters are also delicious hot from the pan with lots of crunchy golden fries (sīb zamīnī sorkh kardeh, page 281). Kotlet was introduced by the tens of thousands of Polish people released from Stalin's hard labor camps during the Second World War who made it across the Caspian Sea. It is now one of the most popular dishes in Iran.

SERVES 4-6

14 oz (400 g) baking potatoes
9 oz (250 g) lean ground beef
1 small onion, coarsely chopped
1 egg, lightly beaten
1 teaspoon sea salt
¼ teaspoon ground turmeric
¼ teaspoon ground cumin
¼ teaspoon cayenne pepper
¼ teaspoon black pepper
Oil, for frying
1 quantity shallow-fried potatoes (page 281)

Cook the potatoes in boiling salted water, then peel and mash. Put the ground beef, onion, egg, salt, and spices in a food processor and process to a paste. Transfer to a bowl and mix with the potatoes by hand, then divide the mixture into 12 portions.

Pour oil in a nonstick frying pan to a depth of about ½ inch (1½ cm). Heat over medium heat until the oil is very hot but not smoking (about 350°F/180°C).

Wetting your hands, shape each portion of the mixture into a tear-shaped fritter. Place the fritters in the hot oil as you go, and cook for 3–4 minutes until brown on one side. Turn the fritters over and cook until brown all over, 3–4 minutes more. You may need to adjust the heat while cooking to keep them from browning too quickly. Once cooked, transfer to a plate lined with paper towels to drain.

Serve hot with the fried potatoes, then enjoy any leftovers with flatbread, pickles, sabzī khordan (page 98), and sliced tomatoes.

Shāmī-ye Bāboli
Beef and Walnut Fritters

Shāmī fritters are made with cooked diced meat (beef or lamb) and boiled yellow lentils or chickpeas. Sometimes mashed potatoes are added. My favorite recipe comes from Bābol, one of the largest cities on the eastern shore of the Caspian Sea. Shāmī-ye bābolī is quite unusual because it includes a lot of fresh herbs as well as walnuts. In spring, it is made with several types of wild herbs that grow by the brooks near rice paddies. When these are out of season, herbs such as mint, dill, and tarragon are used, but you can use any mixture of soft herbs that you fancy. If you have a little leftover cooked meat in the fridge, this is a good way to use it up.

SERVES 4–6

9 oz (250 g) lean beef, diced

1 teaspoon ground turmeric

1 onion, chopped

2 cloves of garlic, finely chopped

9 oz (250 g) baking potatoes

½ cup (1 oz/30 g) mint leaves, coarsely chopped

½ cup (1 oz/30 g) tarragon, coarsely chopped

½ cup (1 oz/30 g) flat-leaf parsley, coarsely chopped

½ cup (1 oz/30 g) cilantro, coarsely chopped

½ cup (1 oz/30 g) dill, coarsely chopped

⅔ cup (1¾ oz/50 g) ground walnuts

2 eggs, lightly beaten

¾ teaspoon sea salt

¼ teaspoon black pepper

Oil, for frying

Put the beef in a small saucepan with the turmeric, onion, and garlic. Cover with cold water. Bring to a boil, then lower the heat and simmer, uncovered, over medium-low heat for 1 hour. Cook off all the water but be careful it doesn't burn.

Cook the potatoes in boiling salted water, then peel and mash. Thoroughly drain the meat, onion, and garlic, transfer to a food processor with the herbs, and process to a paste. Put the paste in a bowl with the potatoes, ground walnuts, eggs, salt, and pepper. Mix well, then divide into 2 inch (5 cm) balls.

Pour oil in a nonstick frying pan to a depth of about ½ inch (1½ cm). Heat the oil over medium heat until very hot but not smoking (about 350°F/180°C).

Wet your hands and flatten each ball into a fritter. Make a hole in the center with your finger and carefully slide each doughnut-shaped fritter into the hot oil. Fry until they are brown on one side, 3–4 minutes, then turn and fry on the other side until cooked, 3–4 minutes more. Transfer each fritter to a plate lined with paper towels to drain. You may need to adjust the heat while cooking to avoid browning them too quickly. Repeat with the remaining balls.

Serve hot or cold tucked into flatbread with fresh herbs (sabzī khordan, page 98) or shallow-fried potatoes (sībzamīnī sorkh kardeh, page 281).

Jūjeh Kabāb-e bā Ostokhūn
Saffron and Lemon Poussin Kebabs

Iranians love cooking and eating outdoors and will make jūjeh kabāb at any opportunity, particularly on our national picnic day (sīzdeh be dar) which we celebrate in April. These juicy morsels of saffron-flavored poussin (jūjeh) can be made with chicken thighs, breasts or breast fillets too. Although eating bone-in jūjeh kabāb from a skewer is a bit messy, I prefer it this way as it is more tender and flavorful.

SERVES 4–6

3 poussins, about 450 g (1lb) each

1 medium white onion

1–2 teaspoons saffron water (page 278)

5 tablespoons plain yogurt

Freshly squeezed juice of two limes or one lemon

1 teaspoon sea salt

1 teaspoon ground white pepper

5 tablespoons oil

Melted butter, for brushing

Pinch of sumac

Lime or lemon wedges, to serve

Using a sharp knife or kitchen scissors cut each bird into 4 portions (2 legs, 2 breasts), then separate the legs from the thighs and divide each breast into 2 pieces. Keep the wings, neck, and backbone for using in a stock.

Grate the onion, then place it in a small piece of cheesecloth and twist to extract the juice. Alternatively, use a small sieve and a spoon to press the juice from the onion.

Mix the saffron water, yogurt, lime or lemon juice, salt, pepper, onion juice, and oil. Pour the marinade over the poussin and mix well. Refrigerate for at least 4 hours or overnight.

Thread the poussin pieces onto skewers, arranging the breasts, legs, and thighs on separate skewers, since the cooking time varies for each.

Preheat your barbecue until the coals are medium-hot. Grill until the skin is crispy, turning every 2 minutes and brushing with melted butter from time to time. The breasts will cook the fastest and the thighs will be the last to cook through. Serve immediately with rice or flatbread, a sprinkling of sumac, lime or lemon wedges, sabzī khordan (page 98), and your favorite green salad.

Bāghālā Ghātogh
Beans with Garlic and Eggs

This simple dish from Gilan is traditionally cooked in an earthenware dish with a dome, similar to a tagine. When I lived in Iran, we visited Gilan often. I never got tired of exploring the diverse food of this region and its marvelous markets, and would always return home with a couple of bags of pale green or pink speckled pāch bāghālā—the local variety of bean. Dried cannellini beans are a good substitute, though I must confess that when I'm hungry and crave this dish (which happens quite often) I usually reach for canned beans. When I'm using canned beans, I cook the garlic and dill base first with a little water, then add the beans so they don't overcook. My cheat version is just as delicious.

SERVES 4–6

1⅓ cups (9 oz/250 g) dried cannellini or butter beans

3½ tablespoons (1¾ oz/50 g) butter

3 tablespoons oil

1 small bulb of garlic, cloves peeled and finely chopped

1 teaspoon ground turmeric

¼ teaspoon ground black pepper (optional)

5 teaspoons dried dill, or ½ cup (1 oz/30 g) fresh dill, chopped

Salt

4 eggs

Put the beans in a bowl and cover with cold water. Allow to soak overnight. Remove the shells by pinching the skin. Rinse, drain, and set aside.

Melt the butter in a medium lidded frying pan. Add the oil and sauté the garlic until almost golden. Sprinkle in the turmeric, pepper, dill, and some salt, then add the beans and cook for 2 minutes while stirring. Pour in enough boiling water to cover the beans by about 1½ inches (4 cm). Cover and simmer gently for about 1 hour or until the beans are soft. Boil off the extra liquid until the beans are barely covered with water.

Make 4 wells in the bean mixture and crack an egg into each hole. Cover the pan and cook over low heat until the eggs are cooked through. You can lightly break up the eggs once the yolks are set. Serve immediately with kateh (page 239), olives, sliced long white radishes (torob) and, if you want to be really authentic, a little smoked fish (māhī dūdī) on the side.

Kūkū Sabzī
Herb Frittata

Kūkū sabzī is another of the green dishes we make for the Nōrūz festival. Traditionally, a kūkū is cooked on the stove and has to be very carefully cut into four equal wedges, then flipped and cooked on the other side. Making kūkū in the oven is a lot easier although many traditionalists will insist that stove-top cooking yields better results. Below I have explained both methods of cooking. I must admit that despite agreeing with the traditionalists, I often take the shortcut.

SERVES 4

⅔ cup (1½ oz/40 g) Persian chives (tareh), baby garlic greens, chives, or curly kale

1 cup (2 oz/60 g) cilantro

1 cup (2 oz/60 g) flat-leaf parsley

1 cup (2 oz/60 g) dill

3½ cups (3½ oz/100 g) spinach or romaine or iceberg lettuce (or use a mixture)

4 eggs

1 tablespoon flour

¾ teaspoon baking powder

¾ teaspoon salt

½ teaspoon black pepper

½ teaspoon ground turmeric

⅛ teaspoon ground nutmeg

¼ teaspoon ground cumin

¼ cup (1 oz/30 g) chopped walnuts (optional)

3 tablespoons barberries (optional)

A handful of walnut halves to decorate (optional)

Oil

Coarsely chop the herbs and spinach. Put the eggs in a food processor and pulse for 5 seconds. Add the flour, baking powder, salt, pepper and spices and pulse for a few seconds to mix well. Add the herbs in batches, pulsing several times after each addition to chop the herbs very finely.

Drizzle 2 tablespoons oil into the mixture (only if using the oven method) and pulse to combine well. Fold in the chopped walnuts and barberries, if using.

Stove-top method: Heat 3 tablespoons oil in a nonstick frying pan over medium-high heat until a small amount of the mixture dropped in the oil sizzles immediately. Add the mixture and gently shake to spread it out evenly. Decorate with walnut halves. After a minute or so, cover the pan and lower the heat. Cook until the mixture is set, has risen a bit, and the underside has lightly browned. Uncover and cut the kūkū into quarters, then gently flip each piece to cook the other side. Add more oil if the pan is dry and cook uncovered until the bottom is lightly browned.

Oven method: Preheat the oven to 400°F (200°C). Grease a 9 inch (25 cm) flan dish with 3 tablespoons oil, making sure the sides are covered. Put the dish in the oven for 4 minutes, or until a little of the herb mixture dropped in the oil sizzles around the edges right away. Pour the mixture into the hot dish and shake gently. Level the top with a spatula. Decorate with walnut halves. Bake for 30–40 minutes or until the walnuts are toasted and the top is golden and crisp.

Kūkū-ye Shīvīd Bāghālī
Fava Bean and Dill Frittata

This is one of several Persian dishes that combine fava beans with dill. According to traditional medical lore, fava beans are a "cold" ingredient so an experienced cook will immediately think of a "hot" ingredient, such as dill, to balance them (see page xv). Whether there's any truth in this or not, dill and fava beans are perfect flavor partners.

Like kūkū sabzī (page 29), this frittata can be served warm or cold, as a side dish, or wrapped in flatbread as a snack. It can be as thick or as thin as you like but I prefer it thicker so I can admire the gorgeous green fava beans when I cut it into wedges. It can also be cooked on the stovetop, if you prefer—follow the instructions for kūkū sabzī. Baby fava beans can be found in farmers' markets, or use fresh or frozen fava beans.

SERVES 4

5¼ cups (1 lb 5 oz/600 g) shelled baby fava beans

4 eggs, lightly beaten

¾ teaspoon salt

½ teaspoon baking powder

½ teaspoon ground white pepper (optional)

2 cloves of garlic, finely chopped

1 tablespoon flour

¾ teaspoon ground turmeric

1 cup (2 oz/60 g) dill, chopped, or 3 tablespoons dried dill

4 tablespoons oil

Use your thumbnail or a small knife to break through the skin of the fava beans, then push the beans out with a gentle squeeze.

Preheat the oven to 375°F (190°C). Combine the eggs with the salt, baking powder, pepper, garlic, flour, and turmeric and beat to combine. Fold the skinned beans and dill into the egg mixture.

Drizzle 2 tablespoons of the oil into an 8 inch (20 cm) flan dish, making sure to coat the sides. Place the dish in the oven for 4 minutes until hot—test by dropping a little of the egg mixture in the oil: if it starts bubbling around the edges, the dish is ready. Carefully pour the mixture into the hot dish. Shake the pan and level the top of the mixture with a spatula. Bake for 15 minutes.

Carefully remove the dish from the oven and brush the remaining oil over the top of the kūkū. Bake for another 15 minutes or until the top is golden brown. Allow to cool a little in the dish, then cut into wedges and serve warm or cold.

Dolmeh-ye Barg
Stuffed Vine Leaves

My Tabrizi family—on my father's side—would always have a pot of stuffed vine leaves simmering on the stove when the year turned, so for me dolmeh will always be associated with Nōrūz. Stuffing vine leaves requires patience but believe me, it's worth the time you spend and is very therapeutic. These freeze rather well, so it's a good idea to make a big batch and save some in the freezer to enjoy later.

SERVES 6-8

60 medium-sized fresh vine leaves or 1 jar of brined leaves

2 medium onions, finely chopped

3 tablespoons oil

½ cup (3½ oz/100 g) long grain rice

¼ cup (1¾ oz/50 g) Persian yellow lentils (or use chana dal; see glossary entry for lapeh, page 306)

½ cup (1 oz/30 g) chives or 2–3 slender scallions, finely chopped

½ cup (1 oz/30 g) finely chopped dill

½ cup (1 oz/30 g) finely chopped mint

½ cup (1 oz/30 g) finely chopped tarragon

½ cup (1 oz/30 g) finely chopped flat-leaf parsley

2 tablespoons dried summer savory (optional)

½ teaspoon ground turmeric

¼ teaspoon ground cumin

1 teaspoon salt

3 tablespoons Greek yogurt

A handful of garlic cloves, peeled

2 tablespoons (1 oz/30 g) butter, cubed

A handful of sour green plums or fresh or frozen gooseberries

If using brined leaves, soak in plenty of water for 1 hour, changing the water a couple of times to remove the salt.

Sauté the onion in 2 tablespoons of the oil until golden. Rinse the rice and the lentils and cook in separate saucepans until they are al dente (check package instructions). Combine the drained rice and lentils with the onions. Stir in the herbs, turmeric, cumin, salt, and yogurt. Drizzle the reamaining 1 tablespoon oil into a medium-sized saucepan and line the base with a double layer of leaves.

To stuff the leaves, lay one on a board, veined side up with the stem end facing you. Put about 2 teaspoons of the filling just above the stem in the middle of the leaf. Fold the right side of the leaf over the filling, then the left side, then roll the leaf up to create a parcel. Continue with the rest of the leaves and stuffing. Lay each parcel in the saucepan seam-side down, packing the bottom snugly to prevent any from bursting during cooking. Add a few garlic cloves on top of each layer.

Scatter the butter on top and pour in enough cold water to just cover. Place a heatproof plate on top of the leaves in the pot to weigh them down. Cover the pot, bring to a boil over medium heat, then lower the heat and simmer gently for 1½ hours.

Remove the plate and sprinkle over the green plums or gooseberries. Simmer gently for another 1–2 hours, until all the water has been absorbed. Keep the heat as low as you can.

Let the dolmeh cool in the saucepan a little, then turn out onto a plate as you would a cake. Serve with plain or garlic yogurt.

Bāghālī Polō
Rice with Fava Beans and Dill

In spring, when the short season for fava beans starts, families buy them in huge quantities to pod and hoard in the freezer for the winter months. Frozen fava beans are particularly useful because freezing makes the removal of their leathery skin much easier. Bāghālī polō is sometimes flavored with a hint of cinnamon, and my mother always sprinkles a little of her rose petal spice mix (adviyeh polōī) between the layers before steaming—the recipe for her mix can be found on page 36.

SERVES 4-6

1¾ cups (12 oz/350 g) white long grain rice

2 tablespoons oil

Flatbread or thick slices of potato for tahdīg (see page 230)

1 cup (2 oz/60 g) coarsely chopped dill

1 tablespoon dried dill (optional)

2¾ cups (10½ oz/300 g) shelled fava beans, peeled (see page 30)

3½ tablespoons (1¾ oz/50 g) butter or ghee

½ teaspoon saffron water (page 278)

Pinch of cinnamon or spice mix (page 36), to garnish (optional)

Prepare and boil the rice according to the instructions for chelō (page 236). Drain in a colander and rinse with lukewarm water.

Heat the oil in a medium-sized lidded pot over medium heat until very hot. Arrange a layer of flatbread or sliced potatoes in the hot oil. Gently mound one-third of the rice in the center of the pot over the flatbread or potatoes. Scatter on one-third of the fresh dill, one-third of the dried dill (if using), and one-third of the fava beans, and repeat until all the rice, beans, and dill are used up. Wrap the lid in a clean dish towel and tightly cover the pot.

Melt the butter or ghee with 2 tablespoons water. Heat the rice over high heat for a couple of minutes or until the side of the pot sizzles when touched with a wet finger. Lift the lid, pour over the butter, and cover again. Lower the heat to very low; steam will soon begin to rise from the rice. Around 30 minutes after the first signs of steam appear, test for doneness by tapping gently on the top of the mound. The rice will "tremble" if it's ready.

To serve, put some of the rice into a small bowl and add the saffron water. Transfer the rest of the rice to a platter and top with the saffron rice. Sprinkle with a pinch or two of cinnamon, or the spice mix, if you wish.

Lift the flatbread or potato tahdīg from the bottom of the pot and place it on a separate plate. Serve immediately with braised lamb shanks (as pictured; page 245), braised chicken (page 243), or fried eggs.

Lubiyā Polō
Rice with Lamb and Green Beans

I would be happy to bet that lubiyā polō is among the top ten favorite dishes of almost every Iranian. My recipe uses my mother's incredible spice mix (adviyeh polōī), the recipe for which has been handed down for generations and is similar to garam masala. During the sixteenth and seventeenth centuries, the Mughal rulers of India were highly influenced by Persian culture, and often had Persian chefs at their courts. These chefs most likely introduced garam masala to Iran when they returned home.

SERVES 4-6

2 cups (14 oz/400 g) white long grain rice

5 tablespoons oil

10½ oz (300 g) green beans, chopped

2 small onions, chopped

7 oz (200 g) boneless lamb shoulder or neck fillet, cut into cubes

¾ teaspoon ground turmeric

¼ cup (2 oz/60 g) tomato paste

1 cup (250 ml) boiling water

½ teaspoon salt

2 medium potatoes, thickly sliced (optional)

1½ tablespoons (¾ oz/20 g) butter or ghee

½ teaspoon saffron water (page 278)

FOR THE SPICE MIX

2 tablespoons dried rose petals

½ teaspoon ground cumin

¼ teaspoon allspice

½ teaspoon cinnamon

Pinch of ground ginger

¼ teaspoon ground cardamom

Pinch of ground nutmeg

Tiny pinch of ground cloves

Wash and soak the rice according to the instructions for chelō (page 236).

Heat 1 tablespoon of the oil in a lidded frying pan and sauté the beans until they begin to caramelize. Remove from the pan and set aside. Add 2 tablespoons of the oil to the pan and sauté the onions until they soften. Increase the heat to high and add the lamb and turmeric. Fry, stirring, for a few minutes until lightly browned. Add the tomato paste and cook for a few minutes.

Return the beans to the pan, add the boiling water and salt, and return to a boil. Cover, lower the heat, and simmer for 20 minutes or until the meat is tender and most of the water has evaporated. The mixture should be fairly dry so it doesn't make the rice mushy.

To make the spice mix, gently heat the rose petals in a small frying pan until the petals are fragrant and beginning to change color. Remove from the heat immediately and transfer to a bowl to stop them from burning. Rub the petals between your palms to powder them. Add the rest of the spices and mix well. Set aside.

Boil the rice according to the instructions for chelō and drain in a colander. Pour the remaining 2 tablespoons oil into the bottom of the rice pot and place over medium heat. Arrange the potato slices in the bottom of the pot. Remove from the heat and add one-third of the rice. Spread half the lamb and bean mixture over the rice and sprinkle with half the spice mix.

Repeat with another third of the rice, and the rest of the meat, beans, and spice mix. Cover with the last third of the rice. Bring the rice from the sides into the center to make a cone shape, so the sides don't get too dry.

Wrap the lid in a clean dish towel and cover the pot. Melt the butter or ghee with 2 tablespoons of hot water in a small saucepan. Return the rice pot to the heat and cook for a couple of minutes on high heat or until the side of the pot sizzles when touched with a wet finger. Drizzle the butter over the rice and cover again. Steam over very low heat for 30 minutes, or until tender and a lot of steam is rising from the rice.

Put a couple of spoonfuls of rice into a bowl and mix with the saffron water. Put the rest in a serving dish and cover with the saffron rice. Serve with chopped cucumbers in yogurt (māst khiyār, page 253) and pickles (torshī, page 262–271).

Kalāneh

Kurdish Scallion Bread with Brown Butter

In the mountainous Kurdish regions in the west of Iran, women make this rustic flatbread with pīchak, a wild plant of the onion family that is foraged in spring. Kalāneh is traditionally quite large, and is cooked on a sāj, a large convex griddle, over an open fire. I make my mini versions with scallions, chives, or wild garlic in a frying pan. My method may not be very traditional, but the bread is still incredibly delicious. Kalāneh keeps well for a day or two, wrapped in paper towels and placed in a plastic bag. Reheat gently in a warm oven when needed.

SERVES 4-6

2½ cups (11 oz/320 g) all-purpose flour

1 teaspoon salt

1 tablespoon oil

About ⅔ cup (160ml) water at room temperature

6 tablespoons (3 oz/80 g) salted butter

2 bunches of scallions, thinly sliced

Put the flour in a bowl and add the salt. Stir well to combine. Make a well in the center and add the oil and half of the water while mixing with your other hand. Gradually add the rest of the water until a very soft dough forms. Stop adding water as soon as the dough stops sticking to your hands. Knead on a lightly floured surface for 10 minutes or until soft and pliable. Shape into a ball and cover with a clean dish towel. Leave to rest for 30 minutes.

In a small saucepan, melt the butter over low heat and cook until it begins to brown. Remove from the heat and set aside.

Lightly flour your surface. Take walnut-sized pieces of the dough and roll into paper-thin circles. Cover half of the circle with the sscallions, leaving a rim just under ½ inch (1 cm). Fold in half over the filling to form semicircles. Crimp or pinch the edges together to seal. Place on a clean dish towel dusted with flour and cover with another dish towel while you prepare the rest.

Place a heavy frying pan over low heat. It's hot enough when a drop of water thrown in it sizzles. Place a couple of the flatbreads in the pan and cook until the underside is dotted with brown spots. Turn over and cook the other side. Remove from the pan and place on a baking tray in a low oven to keep warm while you cook the rest of the flatbreads.

Reheat the brown butter and brush the kalāneh generously on both sides with it. Serve immediately.

Bāghlavā-ye Parchamī Ghazvīnī

Layered Baklava

Baklava is one of the staple sweets of the Persian new year. The cities of Yazd, Gazvin, Kerman, and Tabriz are famous for their baklavas, which always come in a small diamond shape. This recipe hails from Gazvin, which was Iran's capital in the sixteenth century. The name of this version translates as "flag" bāghlavā because of the colors of the layers. To make plain almond, pistachio, or saffron baklavas, you can simply triple the amounts of ingredients for each layer and skip the layering steps. The pastry used is a little thicker than filo, but if you don't want to make your own, store-bought filo works fine. Four or five sheets of filo for each layer is perfect.

MAKES ONE LARGE TRAY

FOR THE PASTRY

1⅓ cups (6 oz/170 g) all-purpose flour
½ teaspoon baking powder
Pinch of salt
3 egg yolks
½ cup (120 ml) whole milk
3 tablespoons oil
Melted butter, for brushing

FOR THE FILLING

Saffron layer—

½ teaspoon ground saffron
2 tablespoons rosewater
2 cups (6½ oz/180 g) ground almonds
1 cup (4¼ oz/120 g) confectioner's sugar
2 tablespoons (1 oz/30 g) butter, cut into small pieces

Cardamom layer –

1 tablespoon ground cardamom
2 tablespoons confectioner's sugar

Lightly oil an 8 by 12 inch (20 by 30 cm) cake pan with straight sides and set aside. Put the flour, baking powder, and salt in a bowl and make a well in the center. Mix the egg yolks, milk, and oil and add this to the flour. Mix with a fork or your fingers until a soft dough forms. Turn out onto a lightly floured surface and knead for 5 minutes with floured hands. If the pastry sticks to your hands, add a little more flour—it should be soft and elastic but not sticky. Shape into a ball and place in a lightly greased bowl. Cover with plastic wrap and leave to rest at room temperature for 90 minutes.

Preheat the oven to 350°F (180°C). Divide the pastry dough into five pieces. Roll one piece on a lightly floured surface as thinly as you can. Stretch it out further with your hands. Carefully lift the pastry into the pan and use a knife to cut off any extra. Brush generously with melted butter, then repeat with another layer of pastry and melted butter.

For the saffron layer, soak the saffron in the rosewater for 5 minutes. Process all the ingredients in a food processor just until the butter is no longer visible—be careful not to overmix. Spread the mixture over the prepared pastry and level with the back of a spoon, pressing down to make it compact. For the cardamom layer, combine the cardamom with the confectioner's sugar and sprinkle evenly over the saffron layer. For the almond

Almond layer –

2 cups (6½ oz/180 g) ground almonds

1 cup (4¼ oz/120 g) confectioner's sugar

2 tablespoons (1 oz/30 g) butter, cut into small pieces

2 tablespoons rosewater

Pistachio layer –

2 cups (6½ oz/180 g) ground pistachios

1 cup (4¼ oz/120 g) confectioner's sugar

2 tablespoons (1 oz/30 g) butter, cut into small pieces

2 tablespoons rosewater

TO FINISH

A handful of slivered pistachios, to decorate (optional)

1 cup (250 ml) water

1¾ cups (12 oz/350 g) sugar

layer, process all the ingredients in the food processor for a few seconds and place over the cardamom layer. Press down firmly with the back of a spoon. For the pistachio layer, process all the ingredients in the food processor for a few seconds and spread over the almond layer. Press down with the back of a spoon.

Cover the pistachio layer with three more layers of pastry, buttering each layer as you go and making sure all the ingredients are tightly packed in the pan. Use a lightly oiled sharp knife to cut the pastry into diamonds or squares, then decorate with slivered pistachios. Bake for 30 minutes or until the pastry is lightly golden. Allow to cool completely.

In a small pan, combine the water and sugar and boil for a few minutes until it's the consistency of maple syrup. Leave to cool slightly, then pour two-thirds over the cold pastry and cover with plastic wrap. Leave to stand overnight. If it looks dry, add the rest of the syrup. (While the baklava is in the pan, it is always possible to add more warm syrup to soften it.) Arrange the baklava on a platter and cover until ready to serve to prevent the pastry from drying out.

Shīrnī Gerdūyī
Walnut Cookies

This is one of the first things I learned to make from my mom. She would prepare the mix and drop it in neat little mounds on the baking sheet, then I would decorate the cookies with chopped pistachios. Her recipe works every time. On festive occasions such as Nōrūz, a large array of sweets, nuts, and fruits are served to guests. The sweets are made in small portions so guests can sample everything on offer. You can make these cookies larger if you like—the taste will be the same, after all.

MAKES ABOUT 40

3 medium egg yolks

½ cup (3½ oz/100 g) sugar

Seeds from ½ a vanilla bean or ¼ teaspoon vanilla bean paste (optional)

2½ cups (9 oz/250 g) walnuts, chopped

1 tablespoon slivered pistachios

Preheat the oven to 325°F (170°C) and line a baking sheet with parchment paper.

Put the egg yolks in a bowl with the sugar and vanilla. Beat with a balloon whisk or hand mixer for 5 minutes until the yolks are a very pale yellow. Fold in the walnuts—the mixture should only just coat them.

Using two teaspoons, place small balls of the mixture, about the size of cherry tomatoes, on the parchment paper, leaving a little space around them. Neaten the shape, then decorate the cookies with the pistachios. Bake for 8 minutes, or until the bottoms are beginning to brown. Turn off the oven and leave the cookies in there to dry for 10 minutes. Store in a tightly covered dish.

Ghōttāb

Almond Turnovers

My mom always made these cute deep-fried turnovers for Nōrūz. After I married she would give me a dish filled with her new year treats, but when I left Iran, I had to learn to make my own. I had always enjoyed baking, but making these turnovers for the first time felt daunting. However, I soon realized the only hard part was crimping the edges—so I often skip this step, and just press the edges together with a fork. If you don't feel like deep-frying, brush the turnovers with melted butter and bake in the oven at 350°F (180°C) for about twenty minutes or until golden.

MAKES ABOUT 24

2 small egg yolks

scant ½ cup (100 ml) plain yogurt

7 tablespoons (3½ oz/100 g) butter, melted and cooled

1⅔ cups (7 oz/200 g) all-purpose flour

¾ cup (3½ oz/100 g) almonds

¾ cup (3½ oz/100 g) confectioner's sugar, plus extra for dusting

1 teaspoon ground cardamom

2 teaspoons rosewater

Oil, for frying

Ground pistachios, to decorate (optional)

Put the egg yolks in a bowl and whisk lightly. Stir in the yogurt, then the butter. Gradually add the flour. When a soft and shaggy dough forms, bring it together into a ball and cover it with plastic wrap. Chill in the refridgerator for 1 hour.

Put the almonds, confectioner's sugar, cardamom, and rosewater in a food processor. Process until the almonds are finely chopped.

Divide the dough in half and roll out one piece on a lightly floured surface to a thickness of ⅛ inch (3 mm). Use a 1½ inch (4 cm) round cookie cutter to cut out circles.

Put a scant teaspoon of the almond filling in the center of each circle, then fold over to form a semicircle. Crimp the edge, or press together with a fork. Cover the prepared turnovers with a dish towel and repeat with the other half of the dough.

Pour the oil into a medium saucepan to a depth of 1½ inches (4 cm) and place over medium heat. The oil is hot enough when a small piece of dough dropped in it rises to the surface in 3 or 4 seconds. Put the turnovers in the oil one by one, making sure you don't overcrowd the pan. You may need to adjust the heat from time to time to keep the temperature constant. Fry until golden, then drain on paper towels. You can either dredge the turnovers in confectioner's sugar while they are still hot, keep them as they are, or dust them with confectioner's sugar once cooled. Decorate with ground pistachios, if desired.

Sōhān Asalī
Caramelized Almond Praline

Sōhān asalī is my favorite new year treat. Sliced almonds, whole hazelnuts, chopped cashews, and even sunflower seeds and sesame seeds work very nicely in this recipe, too. I love folding crushed sōhān asalī into ice cream, or using it to top cakes and desserts for a little crunch and lots of flavor. Always make this in small batches for ease of handling since it will harden quite fast.

MAKES ABOUT 30

¼ teaspoon ground saffron (optional)

2 tablespoons very hot water

2 tablespoons honey

¼ cup (1¾ oz/50 g) sugar

2 tablespoons oil

Pinch of salt

1 cup (3½ oz/100 g) slivered almonds

A few slivered pistachios (optional)

Dissolve the saffron in the water and leave to steep for 5 minutes.

In a small saucepan, combine the honey, sugar, oil, and salt. Add the saffron and stir. Place over medium-low heat and cook without stirring until the caramel begins to bubble and turns golden. Turn the heat down to low.

Add all the almonds at once and stir quickly to coat the nuts. Cook, stirring, until the caramel is golden brown and a sugar thermometer registers 260°F (130°C). Immediately turn off the heat, but leave the saucepan on the stovetop.

Carefully drop spoonfuls of the mixture onto a nonstick or foil-covered baking sheet. If the mixture gets too hard, place the saucepan back over low heat briefly to soften it. Alternatively, pour the mixture onto a foil-covered tray and spread quickly with a spatula. Leave to cool then break into bite-sized pieces and decorate with slivered pistachios, if desired.

Leave the pralines to cool completely before storing between sheets of wax paper in a tightly covered container.

Tūt

Rosewater Marzipan

Almonds have always featured heavily in Persian cooking and confections. "King Khosrow and His Page," a pre-Islamic text written between 591–628 AD, mentions lōzīnag, a kind of almond paste. Today, this almond paste, or marzipan, is enjoyed around new year, and can be flavored with rosewater, orange blossom water, musk willow water, or even jasmine flowers. Keep them in a tightly covered container and make in small batches because they can dry out rather quickly. I sometimes dip them in melted white or dark chocolate—not very authentic but delicious.

MAKES ABOUT 20

1⅓ cups (4½ oz/130 g) ground almonds

Heaped 1 cup (4½ oz/130 g) confectioner's sugar

2 teaspoons egg white, plus more if needed

2 teaspoons rosewater

Green or red food coloring (optional)

Slivered almonds or pistachios, to decorate

Sugar, to dredge

In a large bowl, mix together the ground almonds and confectioner's sugar.

Combine the egg white with the rosewater (and food coloring if using) and pour over the almond mixture. Bring together to form a soft dough, and knead lightly, adding a little extra egg white if needed.

Take small pieces of the dough and shape into ovoids like mulberries. Insert a piece of slivered almond or pistachio at the bigger end to resemble a stem.

Dredge in sugar and pack between layers of wax paper in an airtight container.

SUMMER

The ancient Iranian festival of Tīrgān—the most important event of the summer—is not a celebration of the sun, but instead of water and rain. Without rain, crops would perish, grass would die, cattle would go unfed, and there would be no food to put aside for the hard winter months. Tīrgān honored Tishtar, the god of rain and fertility, and his epic battle with his rival Aposh, the demon of drought. In the shape of a beautiful white horse, Tishtar fought Aposh, who appeared as a giant black horse, for three days and nights, until the Wise Lord finally came to Tishtar's help and allowed the quenching water to flow to the earth again.

Summer produce in Iran is unbelievably diverse. There are soft fruits, such as peaches, apricots, plums, cherries, and sour cherries, as well as juicy white and red Persian mulberries, different types of grapes, and deliciously sweet melons, which we thickly sliced and nibble at the end of a meal. Vegetables are abundant, too—tiny sweet cucumbers, eggplants, zucchini, peppers, sun-kissed tomatoes, green beans, chili peppers, okra, and corn populate the markets, along with vibrant soft herbs.

Summer dishes are lighter, and we usually abstain from very sweet or rich dishes during the hottest months.

According to traditional Persian medicine, one should eat "cooling" food to balance the heat of summer (see page xv). Cooling food isn't necessarily chilled food—though we do eat a lot of chilled soups and salads. Foods such as green lentils, rice, fava beans, cilantro, and most dairy products are considered "cold," while most high-energy ingredients such as nuts or dates, as well as some herbs such as tarragon, and fruits such as persimmons, are "hot" even if they are chilled or frozen.

For us summer is also the time to stock up our pantry for the colder months. This means drying peaches, apricots, sour cherries, green plums, vegetables, and herbs to use through the autumn and winter, making jams and preserves and crushing tart green grapes for verjuice. Traditionally, these activities largely took place outside—as did most of the cooking. Now, since most Iranians live in big cities, outdoor living comes at a premium, but even urban cooks use every inch of space—courtyard gardens, balconies, flat rooftops—in order to bring the outdoors into their summer dishes.

Summer recipes

Ābdūgh Khiyār
Chilled Yogurt and Cucumber Soup

This refreshing soup is the perfect lunch to serve on a hot summer's day. The yogurt needs to be slightly fermented so that it tastes almost like sour cream. Adding sour cream to plain yogurt will give it the tang required—or, for a more authentic flavor, add a small pinch of salt to plain bio yogurt and let it stand in a warm place for a day or two to ferment naturally. Ābdūgh is usually served with broken pieces of crisp flatbread. If it's a very hot day, serve with a few ice cubes floating on the top.

SERVES 4

2 cups (500 ml) plain yogurt

scant ½ cup (100 ml) sour cream

½ cup (1¾ oz/50 g) currants or small raisins

¼ cup (½ oz/15 g) finely chopped chives

¼ cup (½ oz/15 g) finely chopped mint

¼ cup (½ oz/15 g), finely chopped dill

1 teaspoon dried summer savory (or 1 tablespoon fresh, if available)

6 scallions (white part only), chopped

½ cup (1¾ oz/50 g) walnuts, chopped

½ English cucumber, finely diced

3 tablespoons dried rose petals

Cold still or sparkling water, to dilute

Salt

Ice cubes, to serve (optional)

Toasted flatbread, to serve (optional)

Mix the yogurt with the sour cream and leave to stand for 30 minutes. If the currants are very dry, soak them in cold water for 20 minutes to soften. Combine the chopped herbs, currants, scallions, walnuts, and cucumber. Reserve a small handful of this mixture to garnish, then stir the rest through the yogurt.

Add a few of the dried rose petals to your reserved garnish, then crumble the rest of them to a powder. If the petals are not dry enough, heat them in a pan over low heat for a minute, but be careful not to burn them. Add the powder to the yogurt.

Dilute the soup with still or sparkling water as you wish (it can be as thick or as thin as you want). Season with salt, then sprinkle with your garnish. Add some ice cubes if you like, and serve with flatbread dried in a low oven and broken into pieces.

Āsh-e Yakh
Chilled Herb and Yogurt Soup

The first time I tasted āsh-e yakh (which literally means "ice soup") was in my friend Shahla's gorgeous garden on an extremely hot summer day. I was craving something cool and tangy, so when she emerged with bowls of this green-speckled soup with a few ice cubes floating in it, I was thrilled. The very thick base of this soup is often made in large quantities and kept in the fridge to serve on demand. When required, some soured yogurt and a few ice cubes are stirred into it for an instant bowl of refreshing deliciousness. Like ābdūgh khiyār (page 60) this soup tastes best when made with slightly soured yogurt.

SERVES 4

½ cup (3½ oz/100 g) Thai jasmine rice

4 cups (1 liter) water

1 teaspoon salt

1 cup (2 oz/60 g) cilantro, chopped

⅓ cup (¾ oz/20 g) flat-leaf parsley, chopped

½ cup (1 oz/30 g) mint, chopped

½ cup (1 oz/30 g) tarragon, chopped

2½ cups (3 oz/80 g) baby spinach, chopped

½ teaspoon ground white pepper

3 large cloves of garlic, finely chopped or grated

1¼ cups (300 ml) soured yogurt,* thick plain yogurt, or sour cream

Fresh lemon juice, to taste (optional)

Ice cubes, to serve

* See intro note for ābdūgh khiyār on page 60

To make the soup base, put the rice in a saucepan and cover with cold water. Gently rub the grains between your palms to release the starch. Drain the cloudy water and repeat once more. Add the measured water and salt to the rice and place over medium heat. Bring to a boil, then lower the heat and cook for 30 minutes, or until the rice is very soft and breaks easily when pinched between your fingers.

Stir the chopped herbs, spinach, and white pepper into the soup base. Cook for another 30 minutes, stirring from time to time, until the rice has almost disintegrated. Add the garlic and turn off the heat. Allow to cool completely. You can place the soup base in the refrigerator at this point.

When ready to serve, stir in the yogurt or sour cream. Season to taste with salt and more white pepper, and add a little lemon juice if you wish. If the soup is too thick after adding the yogurt, add a little cold water. Ladle into bowls and add a few small ice cubes to each bowl. Serve immediately.

Āsh-e Gojeh Farangī

Tomato, Spinach, and Chili Soup

This hearty soup, chock full of tomatoes, fresh herbs, borlotti beans, and chili peppers, is a specialty of the bountiful Azarbaijan province of Iran. My mother and grandmothers would often make it in summer to take advantage of the juicy red tomatoes when they were at their peak. They would also make huge amounts of robb—a very concentrated tomato paste—at the same time, which would be used to make this soup when tomatoes were no longer available. Āsh-e gojeh farangī is quite spicy, so we spoon cool yogurt over the top to balance the heat. This soup will taste even better the next day.

SERVES 4

3 tablespoons oil or butter

2 onions, finely chopped

1½ teaspoons ground turmeric

6 cups (1½ liters) boiling water or beef stock

¼ cup (1¾ oz/50 g) long grain rice or Arborio rice

1 cup (2 oz/60 g) cilantro, coarsely chopped

1 cup (2 oz/60 g) flat-leaf parsley, coarsely chopped

⅓ cup (¾ oz/20 g) coarsely chopped chives

1 tablespoon dried mint

1 tablespoon dried tarragon (optional)

8 cups (9 oz/250 g) spinach, coarsely chopped

2 cups (500 ml) tomato passata or purée

2 cloves of garlic, finely chopped

3–4 medium tomatoes, cubed

2 medium-hot green chili peppers, finely chopped

1 x 15 oz (425 g) can borlotti, Roman, or cranberry beans, drained

Yogurt, sour cream, or crème fraîche, to serve

1 quantity fried mint (page 276)

Heat the oil or butter in a pot over medium heat and fry the onions until dark brown and caramelized. Add the turmeric and stir for a minute. Add the water or stock and bring to a boil.

Rinse the rice in a small sieve, then add to the pot. Add the herbs, spinach, passata, garlic, tomatoes, and chili peppers. Stir and bring back to a boil. Lower the heat, then cover and simmer gently for 45 minutes or until the soup is thick. Stir from time to time so it doesn't catch on the bottom.

Add the drained beans to the soup and simmer for another 20 minutes. Serve garnished with a dollop of yogurt, sour cream, or crème fraîche and some fried mint.

Māhī bā Somāgh
Grilled Fish with Sumac

Fish is traditionally opened from the backbone in Iran to prevent the flesh from curling while on the grill. This gives the fish a lovely round shape and surface area to absorb marinades and spice rubs. I have given instructions on how to butterfly in the method below, but it does take some patience and skill. If you have a good fishmonger you can ask them to do this for you. Or do as I sometimes do and use thick fillets instead.

SERVES 2

1 large or 2 small sea bream (around 1¾ lb/800 g total)

1 heaped tablespoon sumac

½ teaspoon ground black pepper

¼ teaspoon golpar (ground Persian hogweed seeds, optional)

½ teaspoon sea salt

Juice of ½ a lemon

2 tablespoons (1 oz/30 g) butter, or 2½ tablespoons oil

Lemon wedges (or sour marmalade oranges), to serve

Dill sprigs, to garnish (optional)

To butterfly your fish the Iranian way, lay it on its side and cut along the backbone with a knife, keeping the blade parallel to the bones. Make sure not to cut all the way through the fish's back, since this holds the fish together. Work with the blade to gradually release the flesh on one side, then turn the fish over and repeat with the other side, cutting through the head too. Cut the backbone loose at the top and bottom with a pair of kitchen scissors and pull it out.

Preheat the broiler until very hot. Put the butterflied fish (or fillets) skin-side down on lightly oiled parchment paper on a baking sheet. Mix the spices and salt in a small bowl and sprinkle over the fish. Squeeze over the lemon juice and dot with butter or drizzle with oil.

Place the tray under the broiler on the middle rack. Bake for 8–15 minutes, depending on the thickness of the fish, until the top is lightly golden and the flesh easily flakes with a fork. Remove from the oven and serve warm or cold with a squeeze of lemon or sour orange, and a few dill sprigs. Green salad and buttery rice (kateh, page 239) are good accompaniments.

Kabāb Torsh
Grilled Pomegranate Beef

Whenever I want to escape work or the hectic pace of life in the city, the place I dream of going is Gilan on the shores of the Caspian Sea. I love the friendly people, the gorgeous rice paddies, the emerald-green tea orchards, and the unique markets brimming with fish straight from the sea, fabulous vegetables, and fragrant local herbs. This delicious Gilani kabāb is usually made with beef, though I've used this marinade for chicken thighs, lamb chops, and even a whole rack of lamb with great success.

SERVES 6–8

2 medium onions, grated

¼ cup (60 ml) oil

⅓ cup (80 ml) pomegranate molasses

1 tablespoon finely chopped mint

1 tablespoon finely chopped cilantro

2½ cups (7 oz/200 g) ground walnuts

Juice of ½ a lemon

1 teaspoon sea salt

1 teaspoon ground white pepper

2¼ lb (1 kg) beef or lamb tenderloin, fat and sinew removed, cut into large cubes

3 tablespoons (1½ oz/40 g) butter, melted

¼ cup (1 oz/30 g) pomegranate seeds, to garnish (optional)

Put the grated onion in a small piece of cheesecloth and twist to extract the juice. Alternatively, use a small sieve and press with a spoon to extract the juice. Discard the pulp.

In a bowl, mix the oil, onion juice, pomegranate molasses, herbs, walnuts, lemon juice, salt, and pepper, then add the meat. Rub the marinade into the meat, cover, and refrigerate overnight.

Thread the beef onto metal skewers and grill over medium-hot coals, about 2½ inches (6 centimeters) from the fire, for 3–4 minutes on each side.

Place the skewers on a serving platter and brush generously with melted butter. Garnish with pomegranate seeds and serve with kateh (page 239), walnut and pomegranate marinated olives (page 261), scallions, and pickled garlic (page 271).

Kabāb Kūbīdeh

Ground Meat Kebab

Kabāb kūbīdeh is one of the most popular Persian kebabs and is usually made with a mixture of ground lamb and lean beef. We either eat it with chargrilled tomatoes and a mound of buttered rice, or rolled into flatbread like a wrap. Like other kebabs, it is often sprinkled with sumac to help digest the fatty lamb. These sausage-like kebabs need to be shaped by hand on long flat metal skewers (sikh). We use ¾ inch (2 cm) wide skewers, which you can find online or in specialty shops.

SERVES 4

1 medium onion, grated

9 oz (250 g) extra lean ground beef

9 oz (250 g) ground lamb

1 teaspoon salt

1 teaspoon black pepper

1 teaspoon baking soda

2 teaspoons saffron water (page 278)

4 firm salad tomatoes

8 large mild chili peppers

Melted butter

Plain rice or warm flatbread, to serve

Sliced red onions sprinkled with sumac, to serve

Put the grated onion in a small piece of cheesecloth and twist to extract the juice. Alternatively, use a small sieve and press with a spoon. Discard the juice. Combine the meats and grated onion in a bowl and sprinkle with the salt, pepper, baking soda, and saffron water.

Put disposable gloves on (so you don't turn your hands yellow with saffron) and knead the mixture until it becomes sticky. Alternatively, put the mixture in a food processor and process until well mixed. Cover and chill in the refrigerator for a few hours or overnight. It's very important to chill the mixture so the kebabs don't lose their shape as they grill.

Divide the meat mixture into 4–6 balls (depending on the length of your skewers). Dip one hand in a bowl of cold water and pick up a ball. Hold the skewer in your other hand and lay it on top of the ball. Work up and down the skewer to make a sausage shape, pinching the top and the bottom of the meat to make sure it sticks to the metal. Place the skewers on a tray and chill for an hour or so.

When you are ready to grill, thread the whole tomatoes onto a skewer and the chilies on another, brush with melted butter, and grill until charred on both sides. To avoid dropping them in the fire, try not to turn too often. Remove and cover with foil to keep warm. Fan the fire to make the coals glow red.

Put the skewers on the fire and wait 2 minutes for the meat to set. Turn gently and let the other side cook for a couple of minutes. Brush with melted butter, turn again, and cook for a couple of minutes. Repeat until the meat is cooked through.

Lay the skewer on a platter and, using a piece of flatbread to hold the kebab, gently tug the skewer to release the meat. Garnish with the grilled tomatoes, grilled chilies, and red onion. Serve immediately.

Khoresht-e Holū

Beef and Peach Stew

I make this luxurious fruity khoresht every summer with the season's first peaches. You can also make it in winter with dried peaches, which make a richer stew more suited to the colder months. If you are using dried peaches, soak them in water until plump and add to the meat an hour before it is done. Khoreshts are usually made with lamb, but I personally prefer beef in this dish for its deeper flavor.

SERVES 4

3 tablespoons oil

1 large onion, finely chopped

14 oz (400 g) good-quality stewing beef, cut into large chunks

½ teaspoon ground turmeric

¼ teaspoon ground cumin

¼ teaspoon ground white pepper (optional)

¼ teaspoon ground coriander seeds

2 tablespoons tomato paste

1 small cinnamon stick

½ teaspoon salt

4 firm peaches

1½ tablespoons (¾ oz/20 g) butter

Fresh lemon juice, to taste

Sugar, to taste

½ teaspoon saffron water (page 278)

Slivered or chopped pistachios, to garnish

In a shallow Dutch oven, warm the oil over medium heat and lightly brown the onion. Add the beef and fry until browned on all sides. Stir in the turmeric, cumin, white pepper, and ground coriander, then add the tomato paste and cook for 2 minutes to coat the meat. Pour over enough boiling water to cover the meat and bring back to a boil. Add the cinnamon stick and salt. Turn the heat down to low, cover, and braise for 2 hours or until very tender.

Peel the peaches with a sharp knife, then halve and remove the pits. Cut each peach half into thirds. Melt the butter in a frying pan over medium heat and lightly fry the peach slices until slightly browned on the edges (about 3–4 minutes). This will help them keep their shape once added to the stew.

When the beef is tender, adjust the seasoning with the lemon juice and a pinch of sugar, if needed. If the sauce looks too thick, add some boiling water, or boil off to thicken it if it's too thin. Add the saffron water, then carefully arrange the peach slices over the meat. Spoon some sauce over them, then cover and cook for 5–8 minutes over very low heat until they are soft. Garnish with slivered or chopped pistachios and serve with plain rice (chelō, page 236 or kateh, page 239).

Khoresht-e Bādemjūn
Lamb and Eggplant Stew

This delicately spiced stew is popular all over Iran. People often keep fried eggplants in their freezers so they can whip this up easily on weeknights. It is also delicious made with chicken, and I sometimes make a meatless version using mushrooms and a little more of the spices to even out the flavors. Mushrooms need only a light sauté with the onions before combining with the eggplants so the cooking time is much shorter. When unripe grapes (ghūreh) are out of season we use brined unripe grapes (ghūreh ghūreh). As these are hard to find outside Iran, I use a handful of gooseberries, or flavor the sauce with verjuice or lemon juice instead. I'm hoping a grape vine I've planted in the garden will provide me with authentic sour ghūreh in a year or two.

SERVES 4

4 tablespoons oil, plus more if needed

2 medium onions, finely chopped

1 lb (500 g) lamb neck fillet, lean shoulder, or leg, cut into large chunks

1 teaspoon ground turmeric

½ teaspoon mild curry powder

3 tablespoons tomato paste

1 small cinnamon stick

½ teaspoon salt

¼ teaspoon ground black pepper

2½ cups (600 ml) boiling water

4 small or 8 baby eggplants, peeled and halved lengthways

Pinch of ground saffron (optional)

2 tomatoes, quartered, or a handful of cherry tomatoes

A big handful of unripe grapes (fresh or brined) or gooseberries

Heat 2 tablespoons of the oil in a shallow Dutch oven over medium heat and lightly brown the onions. Add the meat, turmeric, and curry powder and fry until the meat is lightly browned on all sides. Add the tomato paste, cinnamon stick, salt, and black pepper. Cook for a minute, then add the boiling water. Bring back to a boil, then lower the heat and braise, covered, for 2 hours or until the lamb is tender.

Heat the remaining 2 tablespoons oil in a large, lidded frying pan, preferably nonstick. Arrange the eggplant halves in the pan, put the lid on, and cook for 5 minutes. Remove the lid and continue to cook until one side is browned, then carefully turn to brown the other side. Add a little more oil if the pan gets too dry. Alternatively, brush the eggplant halves with oil and roast in a 400°F (200°C) oven for 20–30 minutes.

Season the meat to taste with salt and pepper and add the saffron. Carefully arrange the eggplants and tomatoes over the lamb and top with unripe grapes or gooseberries. The cooking sauce should only just touch the underside of the eggplants so they don't get too mushy. Cover with the lid and braise over low heat for 30–45 minutes or until the eggplants are soft and buttery and the lamb is meltingly tender. Alternatively, cover with foil and bake in the oven at 350°F (180°C) for 1 hour. Serve with plain rice (kateh, page 239, or chelō, page 236).

Khoresht-e Ghormeh Sabzī
Lamb Stew with Dried Limes

This beautiful deep-green stew, flavored with big bunches of fresh herbs, is one of Iran's ultimate comfort foods—many families will have it almost every week. Traditionally, it was only possible to make this dish during the summer months, though now it's eaten throughout the year due to the increased availability of fresh or frozen herbs. Although it has quite complex flavors, it is a favorite with children. When my son was little, he would always watch worriedly as the dish on the table slowly emptied, fearing there wouldn't be any leftovers for him to enjoy the next day. Ghormeh sabzī has many regional variations, but this is my version.

SERVES 4

4 small dried limes

1⅔ cups (3½ oz/100 g) flat-leaf parsley

1⅔ cup (3½ oz/100 g) cilantro

A few small sprigs of fenugreek (optional)

3½ cups (3½ oz/100 g) baby spinach

Tender green inner leaves from 5 small leeks, or a handful of curly kale

5 tablespoons oil

2 onions, finely chopped

1 lb (500 g) lamb neck fillet or lean shoulder, cut into large chunks

1 teaspoon ground turmeric

¾ teaspoon salt

1 x 15 oz (425 g) can borlotti or Roman beans, or red kidney beans, drained

1–2 tablespoons fresh lemon juice (optional)

Cover the limes with hot water and weigh them down with a small plate. Leave to stand for a couple of hours. Strip the leaves from the parsley and discard the stems. Wash the herbs, spinach, and leeks (or kale), and leave to dry.

Heat 2 tablespoons of the oil in a Dutch oven and cook the onions until golden but not brown. Add the lamb and the turmeric and fry until the meat is browned on all sides. Pour over enough boiling water to cover the meat. Bring back to a boil, cover, lower the heat, and braise for one hour.

Working in small batches, finely chop the herbs, spinach, and leeks or kale in a food processor. You could also do this by hand. Put the rest of the oil in a frying pan and fry the chopped greens until they are beginning to darken, but be careful they don't burn. Add the fried herbs to the meat.

Rinse the limes and cut a small slice from the top of each, or make a few slits in their sides, to help release the flavor. Immerse them in the stew and braise for another 30 minutes or until the meat is tender.

Add the salt and drained beans. Continue to braise until the meat is meltingly tender and the sauce has thickened—about 30 minutes. Add the lemon juice (if using) and season with more salt, if required, then cook for 5 minutes. Serve with steamed rice (chelō, page 236 or kateh page 239).

Khoresht-e Bāmiyeh
Lamb and Okra Stew

When I was a child, my siblings and I loved snacking on mouth-puckeringly sour tamarind, which came in big slabs. Before our parents knew it, we would demolish a whole bar. Needless to say, we then had to deal with the resulting tummy ache without complaint. Only a small amount of tamarind is needed here—just enough to give the khoresht its unique sour flavor, without any risk of tummy ache.

This stew from the oil-rich province of Khuzestan has a slightly Indian flavor. Indians employed by the Anglo-Iranian Oil Company had a marked influence on the food in this region. Following the breakout of the Iran-Iraq war in 1980, many war refugees from Khuzestan had to flee and set up home in other Iranian cities, bringing their local cuisine with them.

SERVES 4

4 tablespoons oil

2 onions, finely chopped

1 lb (500 g) lamb neck fillet or lean shoulder, cut into large chunks

1 teaspoon ground turmeric

2–3 cloves of garlic, finely chopped

2–3 tablespoons tomato paste

½ teaspoon cayenne pepper (or as much as you like)

½ teaspoon salt, plus more if needed

1 small cinnamon stick

1 lb (500 g) okra

2–3 tablespoons tamarind paste

Pinch of sugar (optional)

A handful of cherry tomatoes

Heat 2 tablespoons of the oil in a heavy Dutch oven and lightly brown the onions. Add the meat and the turmeric and fry until the meat is lightly browned on all sides. Add the garlic and cook for 2 minutes. Stir in the tomato paste, cayenne, and salt and cook for another 2 minutes. Pour over enough boiling water to completely cover. Add the cinnamon stick and bring to a boil. Lower the heat, cover the dish, and braise for 1½ hours.

Meanwhile, heat the remaining oil in a lidded frying pan and lightly sauté the okra, leaving them whole to avoid any risk of sliminess.

When the meat is really tender, gradually stir in the tamarind paste spoonful by spoonful, tasting as you go to avoid making the sauce too acidic. Season with more salt, if needed, and add a pinch of sugar if you wish.

Add the okra and tomatoes to the meat. Cover and cook over medium-low heat for 30 minutes or until the okra is soft. Discard the cinnamon stick and serve with chelō (page 236) or kateh (page 239).

Estāmbolī
Tomato Rice with Lamb and Fingerling Potatoes

Estāmbolī takes its name from the firm-textured fingerling potato (sīb zamīnī estāmbolī) that reached Iran via Turkey, hence the name "estāmbolī" (from Istanbul). These potatoes have a lovely buttery flavor and keep their shape very well once cooked. This is a popular summer dish, made with fresh tomatoes when they're juicy red and sun-ripened, but can be made with tomato paste (robb) at other times. This recipe calls for lamb, but beef, chicken or even mushrooms can be used in its place.

SERVES 4-6

2 cups (14 oz/400 g) long grain rice

2 cups (500 ml) water

1¾ cups (400 ml) fresh tomato juice

1½ teaspoons flaky regular or smoked sea salt

2 tablespoons oil

1 large onion, chopped

1 teaspoon ground turmeric

1 teaspoon cumin seeds or Persian cumin (zīre-ye polōī)

7 oz (200 g) lamb shoulder, cut into small cubes

7 oz (200 g) fingerling potatoes or 1 large baking potato, diced

1½ tablespoons (¾ oz/20 g) butter

Parsley leaves, to garnish (optional)

Put the rice in a 10 inch (25 cm) nonstick pot, fill the pot with cold water, and swirl the rice around. Pour off the cloudy water and fill with water again. Gently rub the rice between your palms a few times. Pour off the cloudy water again. Drain through a sieve and return to the pot. Add the measured water, tomato juice, and salt and leave to soak for at least 30 minutes.

In a frying pan, sauté the onions in the oil until golden. Add the turmeric, cumin, and lamb and fry until the meat is lightly browned. Fry the diced potato according to the instructions for shallow-fried potatoes (page 281).

Bring the rice to a boil over medium-high heat. Add the meat, butter, and fried potatoes and cook, uncovered, until all the water is absorbed, stirring gently from time to time. Wrap the lid in a clean dish towel and cover the pot tightly. Lower the heat as much as you can and let the rice steam over low heat. The dish is ready when the rice on the side of the pot is beginning to color and get crispy. This will take between 20–30 minutes, depending on the size of your burner. Using a heat diffuser will help prevent the crust (tahdīg) from burning.

Cover the pot with a larger plate and, holding tightly with both hands, invert the rice onto the plate. Garnish with parsley and serve with chopped cucumbers in garlic yogurt (māst khiyār, page 253), a vinegary pickle of your choice (pages 262–274) and/or sabzī khordan (page 98).

Ālbalū Polō
Rice with Sour Cherries

Speckled with tiny sweetened sour cherries, this dish is one of the prettiest and most delicious summer rice dishes of all. The flatbread underneath the rice soaks up the sweet juices from the cherries—I always keep this until last as it provides a lovely sweet finish to the meal. Pitted sour cherries are available frozen from some supermarkets, which makes this dish a lot easier. Sweetened dried or fresh cranberries can be used instead, or even dried cherries and a little lemon juice.

SERVES 4-6

9 oz (250 g) pitted fresh or frozen sour/Morello cherries

5 tablespoons sugar

1 quantity tiny meatballs (page 282)

2 cups (14 oz/400 g) white long grain rice

3 tablespoons oil

Thin flatbread such as lavāsh, cut into pieces

1½ tablespoons (¾ oz/20 g) butter

½ teaspoon saffron water (page 278)

A small handful of slivered pistachios (optional)

Combine the cherries and sugar and set aside for 1 hour. Drain in a sieve set over a bowl. Add enough water to the juices to make a scant ½ cup (100 ml) and bring to a boil. Add the cherries and simmer gently for 10 minutes over low heat.

Prepare and cook the meatballs according to the instructions on page 282. Prepare the rice according to instructions for chelō on page 236, and drain in a colander. Rinse with lukewarm water.

Heat 2 tablespoons of the oil in a heavy pot over medium heat until very hot, and arrange two layers of flatbread pieces in the bottom. Add one-third of the rice, then half of the cherries (but hold the syrup) and half of the meatballs. Repeat until all the rice, cherries, and meatballs are used. Drizzle ¼ cup (60 ml) of the syrup over half of the rice, making sure the other half remains white. Wrap the lid in a dish towel and cover. Melt the butter with 2 tablespoons water and the remaining oil.

Increase the heat and cook for a couple of minutes, until the side of the pot sizzles when touched with a wet finger. Pour over the butter, then cover again. Lower the heat and let the rice steam. Approximately 30 minutes after the first signs of steam appear, gently tap the top of the mound. If it's ready, it will "tremble." Alternatively, after pouring over the butter, the pot can go into the oven at 325°F (170°C) for 45 minutes.

To serve, spoon some of the white rice into a small bowl. Add the saffron water and mix. Transfer the rest of the rice to a platter. Cover with the saffron rice and sprinkle with the pistachios. Break the flatbread tahdīg into pieces. Serve immediately with sālād shīrāzī (page 250) if you like.

Tahchīn-e Shīrāzī
Saffron Rice Cake with Chicken and Eggplant

I found this recipe in Roza Montazemi's *Art of Cooking* when I was at university. Her book was first published in the 1960s, but is still found in most Iranian homes today. This traditional rice dish looks stunning, smells heavenly, and tastes even better. The traditional way of cooking tahchīn involves a long and slow process of steaming the rice over very low heat on the stovetop to form a crisp golden crust. Baking in the oven is more convenient, but it's very important to use a nonstick pot to ensure the cake turns out perfectly. In all honesty, I prefer the good old stovetop method. Once you get the hang of it, it's not difficult at all and produces a much crisper tahdīg (see page 230). The recipe below provides both methods, so you can see which you prefer.

SERVES 4-6

4 chicken thighs on the bone
1 onion, quartered
1 cup (250 ml) water
1 bay leaf
½ teaspoon salt
¼ teaspoon ground turmeric
½ tablespoon peppercorns
2 cloves of garlic
1¼ cups (300 ml) Greek yogurt, lightly beaten
7 tablespoons oil
1 tablespoon fresh lemon juice
3 egg yolks
1½ tablespoons saffron water (page 278)
1 tablespoon (½ oz/15 g) butter
⅓ cup (1¾ oz/50 g) barberries
2 small eggplants
2 cups (14 oz/400 g) long grain rice
1 tablespoon slivered pistachios (optional)

Put the chicken thighs in a saucepan with the onion, water, bay leaf, salt, turmeric, peppercorns, and garlic. Bring to a boil, then lower the heat, cover, and simmer for 30–45 minutes or until the meat is tender. Remove the chicken from the broth and leave to cool, then break it into big chunks, discarding the skin and bones. Remove the aromatics from the broth and discard. Reduce the juices until only 2 or 3 tablespoons are left.

Whisk together the yogurt, 3 tablespoons of the oil, the reduced chicken broth, lemon juice, egg yolks, and saffron water. Pour this over the chicken and marinate for at least 2 hours in the refrigerator. This can stay in the fridge overnight.

Melt the butter in a small saucepan over medium heat and add the barberries. Swirl around for a couple of minutes until puffed up and shiny. Set aside.

Thickly slice the eggplants. Heat 1 tablespoon of the oil over medium heat in a large nonstick frying pan and arrange half of the eggplant slices in the pan. Cover with a lid and cook for a couple of minutes or until the bottom side is browned. Turn over, cover, and cook again to brown the other side. Repeat with the rest of the eggplants and another 1 tablespoon oil.

Prepare the rice according to the instructions for chelō (page 236). Rinse with lukewarm water and drain well. Remove the chicken from the marinade and mix the marinade with the boiled rice.

Preheat the oven to 400°F (200°C) and heat the remaining 2 tablespoons oil in a nonstick ovenproof pot for 4 minutes or until a little of the rice mixture thrown in sizzles. When the oil is very hot, pour in half the rice and marinade mixture and level the surface. Arrange the eggplant slices on the rice and then cover with chicken pieces and half of the barberries. Cover with the rest of the rice. Level the surface and cover tightly with foil.

Bake for 1½–2 hours, or until a golden crust has formed around the edge. Alternatively, place over very low heat on a large burner and steam for about 45 minutes or until the rice around the side of the pot is starting to crisp. Remove the dish from the oven or the stovetop. Cover with a large plate and, holding firmly with both hands, turn the pot and the plate over. Remove the pot carefully and garnish the rice cake with the reserved barberries and slivered pistachios. Serve immediately.

Mīrzā Ghāsemī
Smoky Eggplant Dip

Legend has it that Qasem Khan, a high-ranking government official in Gilan, invented this dish in the nineteenth century upon his return from Russia. For some reason, this wonderful dish was virtually unknown in other areas of the country until a couple of decades ago. Nowadays, it is an enormously popular appetizer all over Iran, served with flatbread, though in Gilan they eat it as a main dish with rice. Grilling the eggplant over charcoal or a wood fire gives it a lovely smokey flavor, but if that is not possible just throw them in a hot oven (400°F/200°C) and bake until the skin is charred, or chargrill the eggplants over a gas flame.

SERVES 4-6

4 large eggplants

5 medium firm tomatoes

3½ tablespoons (1¾ oz/50 g) butter

Half a head of garlic (or a whole head if you wish), finely chopped

1 teaspoon ground turmeric

3 eggs

1 teaspoon smoked sea salt, or to taste

½ teaspoon black pepper, or to taste

Mint leaves, to garnish

Make a shallow cut lengthways on each eggplant. Place the eggplants and tomatoes over a medium-hot charcoal fire and grill until the skin is charred on all sides and the flesh is really soft. Alternatively, you can bake them in an oven preheated to 400°F (200°C) or chargrill over a gas flame. Leave to cool.

Melt half of the butter in a lidded frying pan over low heat and fry the garlic until lightly golden. Add the turmeric and swirl it around for a minute or two. Remove the garlic and break the eggs into the warm oil. Mix lightly and cook until just set, then break them up and fry a little longer. Put a spoonful or so aside to garnish.

Split the eggplants along the existing incision and scoop out the flesh with a spoon. Melt the remaining butter in a pan and add the eggplant flesh. Fry for 5 minutes.

Peel and chop the tomatoes and add them to the eggplants, along with the fried garlic, smoked sea salt, black pepper, and scrambled eggs. Continue to cook for 5 more minutes. Lower the heat, taste and add more salt and pepper, if needed, and cook, covered, for 30 minutes, stirring from time to time until the mixture thickens.

Spoon the dip into a serving bowl and garnish with the reserved egg and a little mint. Serve with warm flatbread or rice.

Kūkū-ye Lūbiyā Sabz
Green Bean and Potato Frittata

Iranians make a lot of food when they are entertaining guests—usually enough to feed a large crowd even if only one or two people are invited. Whenever we had guests over for dinner my mom would always make at least two types of rice—one plain and another layered—and two types of stew. She would also make soup and a few vegetable dishes including this one, which came from my Auntie Husniyah. Our leftovers keep very well and are sometimes even more delicious the next day, so nothing is ever wasted. I love to eat this cold, rolled into bread with sabzī khordan (page 98). If you'd prefer to cook this on the stovetop, use the method for kūkū sabzī (page 29).

SERVES 6-8

6 tablespoons oil

2 medium potatoes, peeled and cut into small cubes

1 lb 5 oz (600 g) green beans, thinly sliced

2 carrots, peeled and diced

1½ teaspoons salt

½ teaspoon baking powder

½ teaspoon black pepper

1 teaspoon ground turmeric

¼ teaspoon ground nutmeg

½ teaspoon ground cumin

1 tablespoon all-purpose flour

6 large eggs, lightly beaten

Chives, to garnish (optional)

Heat 4 tablespoons of the oil in a large nonstick frying pan over medium heat and cook the potato cubes for around 10 minutes until golden brown, stirring from time to time. Remove from the oil, drain on paper towels, and set aside. Fry the beans and carrots in the same oil for about 10 minutes or until they begin to brown around the edges. Leave to cool.

Preheat the oven to 400°F (200°C). Mix the salt, baking powder, and spices into the flour. In a separate bowl, combine the cooked vegetables with the eggs and mix well. Sprinkle in the flour and spice mixture and stir to combine.

Drizzle the remaining 2 tablespoons oil into a pie or flan dish (about 9 inches/25 cm in diameter) and brush around the sides. Place the dish in the hot oven for 4 minutes, or until a little of the mixture dropped in the oil starts bubbling right away. Pour the mixture into the hot oil. Shake the dish and level the top with a spatula. Bake for 30–40 minutes or until the top is golden. Remove from the oven and cool a little before cutting into wedges. Decorate with whole chives, if desired.

Omlet

Eggs in Fresh Tomato Sauce

I have no idea when or where this dish was invented, or how it came to be called omlet (most probably from the French word omelette), but it's the first thing that comes to mind when I'm short on time and feel like a hot meal, whether it be for breakfast, lunch, or dinner. You can add fried onions and garlic, but I like this simplest of versions with just sweet, sun-ripened tomatoes and the freshest eggs you can find.

SERVES 1

1½ tablespoons (¾ oz/20 g) butter

9 oz (250 g) vine-ripened tomatoes, chopped

Sea salt, to taste

2 eggs

Black pepper or red pepper flakes

Melt the butter in a small frying pan over medium heat until it is very hot and beginning to turn brown. Add half of the chopped tomatoes and stir well. Cook for 5 minutes, then add the rest of the tomatoes and continue to cook, stirring from time to time, until the sauce is nice and thick. Use a spoon to crush the tomatoes, if necessary. Stir well and season with salt.

Make two wells in the sauce and break an egg into each. Reduce the heat to medium-low. Cook, uncovered, for about 4 minutes or until the eggs are done to your liking. You could also stir the eggs gently into the tomato sauce and allow to set.

Sprinkle with freshly ground pepper or red pepper flakes and serve immediately with fresh bread—my favorite is tāftūn (page 246)—some sabzī khordan (page 98), and sliced chili peppers or fermented vegetable pickles (page 273).

Kadū Borānisi
Zucchini with Garlic, Yogurt, and Toasted Rose Petals

A borānī is usually served cold, but this classic recipe from my parents' native Azarbaijan is served hot and makes an elegant, light vegetarian meal. The lightly toasted rose petals are typical of the cuisine of Azarbaijan and impart a unique floral aroma to the dish. White zucchini (available from many Middle Eastern grocers) are best for making this as they are firmer and sweeter than the dark green variety.

SERVES 4

6 small zucchini

3 tablespoons oil

1 red onion, finely chopped

5 cloves of garlic, sliced

½ teaspoon black pepper

½ teaspoon salt

½ teaspoon ground turmeric

2 small tomatoes, sliced

Scant ½ cup (100 ml) boiling water

2 tomatoes, chopped

4 tablespoons dried rose petals

Generous ¾ cup (200 ml) yogurt, preferably Greek, lightly beaten

½ teaspoon dried mint

A few drops of saffron water

Cut the zucchini into halves lengthways, then cut each half into three pieces. Heat 1 tablespoon of the oil in a lidded pan over medium heat and fry the zucchini pieces until golden brown on all sides. Remove from the pan and set aside.

Add the rest of the oil to the same pan and fry the onion until golden but not brown. Add the garlic, pepper, salt, and turmeric and cook for a few minutes. Return the zucchini to the pan along with the tomatoes and pour in the water. Cover with a lid and cook over low heat for 30–40 minutes, adding a little more boiling water if it starts to catch on the bottom of the pan. The sauce must reduce to about 3 tablespoons. Adjust the seasoning.

Put the rose petals in a dry pan and toast very lightly until fragrant. As soon as the petals begin to show signs of browning around the edges, transfer them to a plate to cool. Lightly crush between your fingers.

Transfer the zucchini and their sauce to a serving plate. Cover with the yogurt and garnish with the rose petals, mint, and saffron water. Serve hot with warm flatbread and sabzī khordan (page 98).

Nūn-o Panīr-o Sabzī Khordan
Bread, Cheese, and Herbs

Nūn-o panīr used to mean "something humble." Humble as it may be, bread and cheese (nun-o panir) paired with fresh herbs (sabzī khordan) is a much loved dish, enjoyed for breakfast, as a quick snack, or as a light meal on a hot summer day.

While I cannot give a recipe as such, I can advise how to serve nūn-o panīr-o sabzī khordan the Persian way. Sabzī khordan, literally translated as "greens for eating," is an indispensable component of any proper Iranian meal. It's a medley of soft aromatic herbs such as mint, Persian basil, red basil, cilantro, flat leaf parsley, dill, Persian chives, as well as radishes and scallions. Just combine whichever fresh herbs you have on hand, using equal measures of each.

Persian cheeses (most of them unnamed) are made from cow, sheep, goat, or buffalo milk. Cheese is usually aged in brine in ceramic pots and even sheepskins. The flavor of the crumbly and salty white English cheese, Cheshire cheese, is similar to Līghvān, a very popular sheep's cheese from eastern Azarbaijan. Greek Feta, or any mild and soft or crumbly sheep's or goat's cheese, are also good substitutes.

According to Persian medical lore, cheese must be eaten with walnuts to be good for the body—and, happily, this is a delicious combination, whether it's true or not. It is best to soak the walnuts in plenty of very lightly salted warm water for a couple of hours to soften the nuts and remove the bitterness from their skin. It also makes them crisp and crunchy.

To bring this all together, warm some flatbread (lavāsh, tāftūn, barbarī, Indian naan, or pita) in the oven for a couple of minutes and arrange in a basket. Bring the bread to the table with the cheese, your soaked walnuts and sabzī khordan, along with a few sliced cucumbers and tomatoes, and encourage everyone to make their own sandwich wraps.

I wouldn't serve nūn-o panīr-o sabzī khordan as an appetizer since it's quite filling. Leave it instead for a long summer evening spent with friends or family when you want to serve something casual for people to nibble on. Along with a few other small dishes such as mīrzā ghāsemī (page 90), kūkū sabzī (page 29), māst khiyār (page 253), zeytūn parvardeh (page 261) and a glass or two of your favorite beverage, this humble dish can easily transform into a feast.

Nargesī
Daffodil Spinach Frittata

In classical Persian poetry, narges (daffodils) are often used as a metaphor for beautiful eyes. This gorgeous spinach frittata is named after the flower because it is served with a sunny side up egg in the middle. Eat it with sliced radishes and plenty of warmed flatbread or crusty bread to scoop up the spinach and eggs. If you are lucky enough to have leaf sorrel in your garden, throw in a handful to add a slightly tart note.

SERVES 4

1 lb (500 g) fresh spinach
3½ tablespoons (1¾ oz/50 g) butter
1 red onion, thinly sliced
2 cloves of garlic, finely chopped
Juice of ½ a lemon
Salt and pepper, to taste
4 eggs
Lemon, to serve

Wash and roughly chop the spinach, then put the wet leaves in a saucepan. Cover and cook for a few minutes over medium heat to wilt the leaves, then drain well.

Melt the butter in a large frying pan over medium heat and cook the onions until golden brown. Add the garlic and fry until fragrant and lightly golden. Add the drained spinach and lemon juice and season with plenty of salt and black pepper. Cover and cook for a few minutes. Remove the lid, stir well, and cook for a few more minutes until nearly dry.

Divide the mixture into four in the pan. Make a well in the center of each portion and break an egg into each well. Cook over medium-low heat for about 4 minutes or until the eggs are set to your liking. Carefully transfer each portion to a plate. Alternatively, lightly mix three of the eggs into the spinach and break the fourth in a well in the middle, then take to the table in the same dish it was cooked in. Serve immediately with a squeeze of lemon.

Fālūdeh Shīrāzī
Rosewater Sorbet with Rice Noodles and Lime

This frozen treat is a speciality of Shiraz, where we lived for a couple of years when I was a child. My dad would often take us to a lovely fālūdeh shop on the main street where it was served in pretty handmade glass bowls. As a child I was fascinated with the beauty of this dessert. In the pre-Islamic courts of Persian kings, a chilled dessert named pālūdag (the ancient form of fālūdeh) was made from snow specially delivered from the mountains. The refreshing sorbet must be kept slushy to keep the noodles crunchy.

SERVES 4-6
1¾ cups (400 ml) water
Scant 2 cups (13½ oz/380 g) sugar
½–1 tablespoon rosewater
7 oz (200 g) dry thin rice noodles, cut into 1 inch (2½ cm) pieces using kitchen scissors
Freshly squeezed lime juice
Sour cherry syrup or raspberry coulis, to serve

Put the water and sugar in a saucepan and bring to a boil. Stir until the sugar is well dissolved, then cook gently for 5 minutes and leave to cool. Add the rosewater to the cooled syrup and stir. Put the mixture in the freezer and chill for 4–6 hours or until the syrup is semi-frozen.

Place it in a blender or food processor and blend to break up the ice crystals. Alternatively, put the mixture in an ice cream maker and churn according to the manufacturer's instructions for sorbet. Pour back into a plastic container and store in the freezer until needed.

Bring a pot of water to a boil and cook the noodles until they are very soft. Drain and rinse well with cold water. Cover and chill in the fridge until you are ready to serve.

Remove the sorbet from the freezer 20 minutes before serving to allow it to soften. When ready to serve, set out a large bowl and fill it with half water and half crushed ice. Drop the noodles into the icy water and stir around. They will begin to freeze and turn very white and crunchy. When they are completely white, drain well and fold them into the sorbet. Serve immediately with the lime juice and some sour cherry syrup (as they do in Shiraz) or with raspberry coulis—not traditional, but very delicious.

Bastanī-ye Akbar Mashtī

Rosewater Ice Cream with Pistachios

This ice cream is named after Akbar Mashtī, who opened Tehran's first ice cream parlor in the late nineteenth century. In his day, ice had to be delivered from the mountains and stored deep underground to keep it from melting. In summer my grandfather, whose office was close to Akbar Mashtī's ice cream parlor, often came home with a huge block of this ice cream wrapped in wax paper. The ice cream was flavored with rosewater and had pistachios and chunks of frozen cream in it. I usually use good-quality store-bought vanilla custard to make my ice cream but you can make your own according to the basic recipe below if you prefer.

SERVES 4

1½ cups (350 ml) heavy cream, well chilled

Scant ½ cup (3 oz/80 g) sugar

1¼ cups (300 ml) prepared vanilla custard (store-bought or made according to recipe below), well chilled

2 tablespoons rosewater, or to taste

Scant ½ cup (1¾ oz/50 g) unsalted pistachios, coarsely chopped

FOR THE VANILLA CUSTARD

3 egg yolks

Seeds from one vanilla bean

3 tablespoons sugar

1 tablespoon cornstarch

1 tablespoon all-purpose flour

1¼ cups (300 ml) milk

Put 3 tablespoons of the cream in a small ziplock bag and spread into a thin layer. Freeze flat in the freezer. Whip the rest of the cream until very soft peaks form. Add the sugar and whip gently until the sugar is dissolved. Mix the custard* with the rosewater and gradually fold it into the whipped cream.

To churn in an ice cream maker, follow the instructions for your machine. Alternatively, put the mixture in two large ziplock bags and freeze flat. Once firm, break the ice cream into chunks and put in the bowl of a food processor in two batches. Whizz until soft and creamy.

Break the frozen sheet of heavy cream into small pieces and fold into the ice cream with three-quarters of the chopped pistachios. Transfer to a tub and keep in the freezer until required. To serve, spoon into small bowls and garnish with the rest of the chopped pistachios.

* To make your own custard, beat the egg yolks with the vanilla, sugar, cornstarch, and flour until very pale. Heat the milk in a saucepan until it begins to come to a boil. Pour the hot milk over the egg mixture, beating constantly, then return the mixture to the saucepan and cook over low heat until thickened. Leave to cool, covering the surface with plastic wrap to stop a skin from forming. Chill in the refrigerator until use.

Āb Tālebī bā Golāb
Melon and Rosewater Smoothie

Iran is one of the largest melon producers in the world. We grow several varieties, including honeydew, cantaloupe, and watermelon, all of which are quite cheap to buy. When they are in season people usually have at least one melon in the fridge to enjoy on demand. On hot summer days, ice-cold melon juice scented with rosewater is often offered, sometimes with a scoop of ice cream floating on top. Frozen chopped melon from the supermarket is perfect for this recipe if you can't find a fresh one. Allow it to partially defrost before blending.

SERVES 4
1 large honeydew or cantaloupe
½–1 tablespoon rosewater
Crushed ice
Sugar, to taste
Vanilla ice cream, to serve
(optional)

Cut the melon in half and remove the seeds with a spoon. Scoop out the flesh and put in a blender with the rosewater and a few tablespoons of crushed ice and process until smooth. Taste, and add a little sugar if you like it sweeter. Blend for a few seconds to dissolve the sugar and pour it into four glasses. Add a scoop of ice cream to each glass if you like, and serve immediately with long spoons.

AUTUMN

Autumn is a season of bounty. Throughout Iran, the markets abound with quinces, squash, pomegranates, as well as fresh pistachios, walnuts, and barberries. Whenever I think of autumn, I picture my mother drying mounds of cauliflowers, carrots, Jerusalem artichokes, celery, cucumbers, and herbs in order to make her fabulous torshī (pickles), fermented vegetables (shūr), or cucumber pickles (khiyār shūr). These would be stored for the sparser winter months, to brighten up the table at mealtimes.

Fall in Iran begins with a month dedicated to Mithra, the ancient Persian warrior god. Venerated as the protector of truth, he was believed to watch over the cattle, the harvest, and the waters. The word "Mithra," now pronounced as Mehr, has come to mean both "love and compassion" and "the Sun." The festival of Mehregān has been held in his honor for millennia. Today, Iran's Zoroastrians hold the Mehregān festival at their fire temples in Yazd, Kerman, and Tehran, celebrating with prayers and a special spread that includes a bread made with seven different seeds and cereals (lurag), a mixture of seven types of nuts and dried fruits (ājīl), and seven different types of fruit. The festival is also being revived by secular Iranians—both in Iran and abroad—despite it being frowned upon by the hardline Islamic establishment.

As we draw close to the very last days of fall, we prepare for another festival, Yaldā, which is one of the most widely celebrated events in Iran. Yaldā falls on the evening before the Winter Solstice, and is the last and longest night of the year. It is a family occasion, very closely tied to food, much of which has symbolic meaning. On the evening of Yaldā the house will be decorated with candles and huge bowls filled with pomegranates, nuts, and watermelons.

The pomegranates and watermelons symbolize fire and the warmth of the sun, which will win its battle against darkness as the days grow longer. People stay up very late on Yaldā, eating, drinking, reading poetry, and telling their fortunes with the Dīvān-e Hāfez, a collection of poems in praise of love, beauty, and wine from the fourteenth century. The feasting will often continue until the first rays of the new sun appear on the horizon, bringing autumn to an end.

Autumn recipes

Gildik Āshi

Rosehip Soup

This thick, luscious soup is virtually unknown outside northwestern Iran. If you have a wild rose in your garden, or live near the countryside, collect the rosehips in autumn and freeze them so you can make this soup whenever you fancy. Dried rosehips are available from health food stores and online, but need to be soaked for at least two days before they can be used. Rosehips are a very rich source of vitamin C and are also delicious in herbal teas, jams, and marmalades.

SERVES 4

½ quantity tiny meatballs (page 282)

2½ cups (9 oz/250 g) fresh rosehips

3 tablespoons oil

2 large onions, chopped

½ teaspoon ground turmeric

3 tablespoons Thai jasmine or Arborio rice

½ teaspoon salt

¼ cup (1 oz/30 g) dried apricots, coarsely chopped

3 tablespoons dried sour cherries or dried cranberries

scant ½ cup (1½ oz/40 g) walnut halves

1 x 15 oz (425 g) can black-eyed peas, drained

scant ½ cup (1½ oz/40 g) Persian soup noodles or udon noodles, broken into pieces

Salt and black pepper

Pinch of sugar

1 quantity fried mint (page 276)

Prepare and cook the meatballs according to the recipe on page 282 and set aside. Wash the rosehips thoroughly, then halve them and place in a saucepan. Cover with water and cook over medium heat for 20 minutes. Allow them to cool a little, then purée in a food processor for a few seconds. Pass the mixture through a sieve and discard the seeds.

Heat the oil over medium heat and fry the onions until golden brown, 10–15 minutes. Add the turmeric and cook for a minute or so. Remove 2 tablespoons to use as a garnish, then add the rice, salt, apricots, cherries, and walnuts to the pan and pour over 4 cups (1 liter) cold water. Bring to a boil, uncovered.

Add the meatballs and the rosehip purée. Lower the heat, cover the pot, and simmer gently for about 45 minutes, stirring from time to time. Add some boiling water from the kettle if the soup gets too thick.

Reserve a few of the beans for the garnish, and add the rest to the pot along with the broken noodles. Cook for 10–15 minutes until the noodles are very soft. Taste, season with salt and pepper, and add a pinch of sugar if the soup is too sour. Ladle into four bowls and garnish with the beans, fried onions, and fried mint.

Āsh-e Māst

Herb and Chickpea Soup

Āsh-e māst was my father's favorite soup. My mother always made it when one of us had a cold, and so my father would sometimes pretend to be coming down with something in order to get a bowlful. Like most thick Persian soups, you can make this vegetarian—as it always was in our house—or use meat stock and drop in tiny meatballs as in the recipe for rosehip soup (page 114).

SERVES 4

¼ cup (60 ml) oil

3 medium onions, chopped

1 tablespoon ground turmeric

6 cups (1½ liters) boiling water

¼ cup (1¾ oz/50 g) Thai jasmine or Arborio rice

1 x 15 oz (425 g) can chickpeas, drained

⅔ cup (1½ oz/40 g) cilantro, coarsely chopped

⅔ cup (1½ oz/40 g) flat-leaf parsley, coarsely chopped

1 tablespoon dried summer savory or 2 tablespoons fresh (optional)

10 cups (10½ oz/300 g) spinach, coarsely chopped

Salt and black pepper

1 cup (250 ml) plain yogurt, sour cream or crème fraîche

Black pepper and/or red pepper flakes, to garnish

Heat the oil in a lidded saucepan and fry the onions over medium heat for 10–15 minutes, until golden brown. Add the turmeric and swirl around until it becomes fragrant. Remove a tablespoon of the fried onions for the garnish.

Add the water and rice to the rest of the fried onions and bring to a boil. Lower the heat and simmer for 30 minutes.

Add the chickpeas, herbs, and spinach and bring to a boil again. Lower the heat and simmer for 40 minutes. Season with salt and pepper.

Beat the yogurt and stir all but ¼ cup (60 ml) into the soup. Heat through gently, but don't boil or the yogurt will curdle. Serve immediately garnished with the rest of the yogurt, the reserved onions, and a little black pepper and/or red pepper flakes.

Adasī bā Reshteh
Green Lentil Soup with Noodles

Adasī is one of the few warm dishes travelers are likely to find for breakfast at the makeshift cafés that line roadsides throughout Iran. Usually served along with brown butter fried eggs (page 206), cheese, flatbread, clotted cream, and honey, this makes a very hearty morning meal, but is also perfect for lunch or a light supper. The following recipe hails from Saqqez, an ancient city tucked away in the Kurdish mountains and uses Persian soup noodles (reshteh) as a thickener. My Japanese friends in Iran sometimes use udon noodles instead, which make a very good substitute if you can't find reshteh.

SERVES 4

2 tablespoons oil

1 onion, finely chopped

½ teaspoon ground turmeric

½ teaspoon ground black pepper

¼ teaspoon ground cumin

2 tablespoons tomato paste

1¼ cups (9 oz/250 g) green lentils

6 cups (1½ liters) water

½ teaspoon salt, plus more if needed

1¾ oz (50 g) Persian soup noodles or udon noodles

1 quantity fried mint (page 276)

Heat the oil in a saucepan over medium heat and add the chopped onion. Cook until golden brown, stirring from time to time, then add the spices and tomato paste and cook for a minute or two. Add the lentils, measured water, and salt and bring to a boil. Reduce the heat to low, cover, and simmer gently for 30 minutes, until the lentils are cooked through.

Break the noodles into 4 inch (10 cm) lengths and add to the pot. Stir well to separate. Cook for 20 minutes or until the noodles are very soft and the soup has thickened. Taste and add more salt if needed.

Stir half of the fried mint into the soup, then ladle into bowls and garnish with the rest. Serve immediately.

Māhī-ye Shekampor-e Jonūbī
Southern-Style Baked Fish

Though stuffed fish recipes vary a great deal from one place to another in the coastal regions along the Persian Gulf, they are always rich with garlic and spices. This recipe uses barberries and raisins, but the stuffing is delicious without them as long as it is well spiced. Tamarind gives the stuffing a distinctive sour taste. The amount you use largely depends on how concentrated your paste is. The tamarind that we get in Iran has to be soaked and sieved before use and I find this much tastier than the dark ready-made paste, but use whichever you like or is available. For this dish I like to use sea bass, sea bream, red mullet, or snapper.

SERVES 6-8

2 medium sea bass, scaled

¾ teaspoon sea salt flakes, crushed

5 tablespoons oil

1 onion, chopped

1 cup (2 oz/60 g) cilantro, finely chopped

A large sprig of fenugreek, finely chopped (optional)

3–4 cloves of garlic, finely chopped

¼ teaspoon cayenne pepper, or more

¼ teaspoon ground black pepper

¼ teaspoon ground coriander

¾ teaspoon ground turmeric

2 tablespoons barberries or pomegranate seeds

2 tablespoons currants or chopped raisins (optional)

1–2 tablespoons tamarind paste

1 tablespoon all-purpose flour

Lime wedges, to serve (optional)

Preheat the oven to 350°F (180°C). Rinse the belly of the fish and pat dry with paper towels. Sprinkle the inside and the skin of the fish with ½ teaspoon of the salt and set aside.

Heat 2 tablespoons of the oil in a frying pan and cook the onions until lightly golden. Add the cilantro, fenugreek, garlic, cayenne, black pepper, coriander, and ½ teaspoon of the turmeric. Cook for 5 minutes over low heat, until the mixture is fragrant and the garlic is soft, then add the remaining salt and the barberries and raisins and mix well. Add the tamarind and cook for 2 minutes. Remove a tablespoon to use as a garnish.

Cut six pieces of kitchen twine and lay three pieces on a lightly oiled baking dish. Gently lay a fish on top, stuff the belly with half of the mixture and tie with twine to hold it all together. Repeat with the other fish.

Mix the flour with the remaining ¼ teaspoon turmeric and a pinch of salt. Lightly dust the fish with the flour mixture. Drizzle over the remaining oil and bake in the oven for 40 minutes, until the skin is golden. Baste with the oil from the bottom of the dish once or twice as they cook. Garnish with the reserved stuffing and lime wedges, and serve with buttered chelō (page 236).

Māhī Aflātūnī

Platonic Fish Stew

According to Zari Khavar, the amazing woman who wrote the first ever book on the cuisine of Gilan in the 1980s, this fish stew originated in a small village called Shalman. Zari is my ultimate authority on Gilaki cuisine, but it took me quite a few years to make up my mind to try her recipe for Platonic fish, because the amount of souring agents in the recipe sounded insane. When I finally made the dish, however, it was so delicious I couldn't stop eating it. Verjuice is available from Middle Eastern grocery stores and online. Wine is not used in Persian cooking, but in this recipe you could use white wine instead of the verjuice.

SERVES 4

2 tablespoons all-purpose flour

½ teaspoon salt

2 medium sea bream, or 1 large grey mullet, deboned and filleted

¼ cup (60 ml) oil

½ cup (120 ml) pomegranate juice*

½ cup (120 ml) verjuice or dry white wine

½ cup (120 ml) fresh lemon juice

½ teaspoon ground black pepper

½ teaspoon cinnamon

Pinch of ground nutmeg

2 tablespoons tomato paste

Dill sprigs and chives, to garnish (optional)

*To make fresh pomegranate juice, deseed two pomegranates and process in a food processor. Leave the juices to drain in a sieve over a bowl. Press the pulp with the back of a spoon to draw as much juice as you can and discard the pulp.

Mix the flour and salt and sprinkle over the fish fillets. Heat the oil in a large frying pan over medium heat, shake the excess flour from the fillets, and fry on both sides until golden.

Mix the rest of the ingredients together and pour over the fish. Cover and cook gently over low heat for about 15 minutes or until the sauce has thickened to your liking. If the sauce is too thick, add a splash of boiling water from the kettle and cook for a few minutes longer. Garnish with dill sprigs and chives, if using, and serve immediately with kateh (page 239), olives, and sliced radishes.

Khoresht-e Karafs

Lamb and Celery Stew

When huge heads of celery crowned with emerald green leaves start appearing in the market, it's time to make this delectable stew. A British friend of mine who lived in Iran for a couple of years fell in love with this dish, but could never find it on restaurant menus. Staples of home cooking like this are rarely on offer in Iranian restaurants, probably because everybody thinks they taste better at home. I recommend making this a day or two before you mean to serve it, making it perfect for stress-free dinner parties. Just leave it to sit in the fridge, then reheat gently before serving.

SERVES 4-6

1 large or 2 small heads of celery, including any tender leaves

1⅔ cups (3½ oz/100 g) flat-leaf parsley

1⅓ cups (3 oz/80 g) mint

6 tablespoons oil

2 onions, finely chopped

1 lb (500 g) lamb neck fillet or lean shoulder, cut into chunks

1 teaspoon ground turmeric

1 tablespoon all-purpose flour

1 teaspoon ground celery seeds (optional)

½ teaspoon celery salt

1–2 tablespoons fresh lemon juice

¼ teaspoon sea salt

Mix together the celery leaves and herbs and process in a food processor in two batches. Alternatively, finely chop by hand.

Heat 2 tablespoons of the oil in a heavy pot or Dutch oven and lightly brown the onions. Add the lamb and turmeric and fry until lightly browned on all sides. Pour over enough boiling water to cover the meat by about ¾ inch (2 cm). Bring to a boil, then lower the heat and simmer gently, covered, for 1 hour.

Cut the celery stalks into ¾ inch (2 cm) pieces. Heat 2 tablespoons of the oil in a frying pan over medium heat and add the celery and 2 tablespoons of water and cover. Cook, stirring occasionally, until almost soft and slightly golden around the edges. Remove from the pan and set aside.

In the same pan, heat the remaining 2 tablespoons oil and add the chopped herbs. Sprinkle on the flour and celery seeds, if using, and stir. Sauté until the leaves darken in color a little— around 5 minutes—but be careful they don't burn.

Add the herbs, celery, and celery salt to the lamb and stir through. Bring to a boil, then reduce the heat to very low, and simmer for 1½ hours or until the meat is really soft and the sauce is thick. Add the lemon juice, to taste, and season with salt. Cook for another 5 minutes and serve with chelō (page 236) or kateh (page 239).

Khoresht-e Havīj
Lamb and Carrot Stew with Brined Grapes

This comforting malas (mildly sweet and sour) khoresht is traditionally flavored with ghūreh ghūreh—unripe grapes preserved in either brine or verjuice. If neither is available, we use lemon juice to add acidity to the sauce. I have also improvised with fresh or frozen gooseberries with surprisingly good results. Up until the middle of the twentieth century, the carrots grown in Iran were mainly yellow or purple. The orange carrot imported from Europe, still sometimes called "European carrot," quickly ousted its native cousins, but my grandma always made this dish with yellow carrots.

SERVES 4-6

3 tablespoons oil

1 onion, finely chopped

14 oz (400 g) boneless lamb shoulder, leg, or neck fillet, cut into large chunks

½ teaspoon ground turmeric

Pinch of cinnamon

¼ teaspoon ground cumin

2 tablespoons tomato paste

½ teaspoon salt

1½ tablespoons (¾ oz/20 g) butter

1 lb (500 g) carrots, cut into batons

½ teaspoon saffron water (page 278)

4 heaped tablespoons ghūreh ghūreh or gooseberries (optional)

Heat the oil over medium heat in a heavy-bottomed pot and lightly brown the onions. Add the meat, turmeric, cinnamon, and cumin and fry until the meat is lightly browned on all sides. Stir in the tomato paste and salt and cook for another 2 minutes. Pour over enough boiling water to cover the meat by about ¾ inch (2 cm) and bring to a boil. Turn the heat to low, cover the pot, and braise for 1½ hours or until the meat is tender.

Meanwhile, melt the butter in a large lidded frying pan and lightly fry the carrot batons until they begin to caramelize around the edges. Set aside.

Add the meat and its sauce to the carrots, along with the saffron water and a little boiling water if the sauce is too thick. Season, then scatter the ghūreh ghūreh or gooseberries on top and bring to a boil. Lower the heat, cover, and allow the khoresht to simmer until the carrots are very soft and the meat is meltingly tender. Serve with chelō (page 236) or kateh (page 239).

Khoresht-e Khelāl
Jeweled Sweet and Sour Lamb

In 1980—the year after the Iranian Revolution—I was living in Kermanshah studying for my high school diploma. It was in that beautiful city that I first ate this extravagant stew at a classmate's house. Khoresht-e khelāl used to be a dish for special occasions since making it took several days. This provided an excuse for the women of the family to get together and enjoy each other's company, drinking endless small glasses of tea, and snacking on miniature sweetmeats as they shelled, soaked, and skinned almonds, slivered the nuts, and spread them out to dry. Barberries collected from the mountains had to be picked over carefully, rinsed, and dried. All these things are now available pre-prepared, so there's little excuse for such lengthy preparations—or for those joyous get-togethers.

SERVES 4-6

1 cup (3½ oz/100 g) slivered almonds*

2 dried limes

2 tablespoons oil

2 small onions, finely chopped

1 lb (500 g) boneless lamb neck fillet or lean shoulder, cut into large cubes

1 teaspoon ground turmeric

2 tablespoons tomato paste

½ stick cinnamon

1 cup (5 oz/150 g) barberries

2 tablespoons (1 oz/30 g) butter

½ tablespoon rosewater (optional)

1 teaspoon saffron water (page 278)

Sea salt, to taste

Sugar, to taste

Parsley, to garnish (optional)

*To make your own slivered almonds, soak blanched almonds in warm water for a few hours to soften. Drain well and slice with a sharp knife. Use them as they are, or spread them on paper towels to dry. Freshly sliced almonds need only a few minutes to cook in the stew.

Cover the slivered almonds with cold water and leave to soak for 30 minutes, then rinse well in a sieve. Cover the limes with hot water, then cover with a plate so they remain immersed.

Heat the oil in a heavy-bottomed saucepan and fry the onions over medium heat, stirring frequently, until they begin to color. Increase the heat to high, add the lamb and turmeric, and fry until the meat is well browned on all sides. Add the tomato paste and cook for a minute or two. Pour in enough boiling water to cover the meat by a fingertip and add the cinnamon. Cover and simmer over low heat for 1 hour.

Rinse the limes and cut a small slice from the top of each or make a few slits on the sides so they can release their flavor. Tuck them into the stew, along with the drained almonds. Cover and simmer for 30 minutes.

Pick over the barberries and rinse with cold water. Drain well and leave to dry. Melt the butter in a small saucepan and fry them for a few seconds over low heat until they puff up.

When the lamb is very tender, add the barberries, rosewater (if using), and saffron water. Stir, taste, and add salt, if needed. Adjust the amount of the sauce by boiling off the extra liquid or adding a little boiling water. The sauce shouldn't be too thin. Add a pinch of sugar if the stew tastes too sour. Garnish with parsley, if using, and serve with plain rice (chelō, page 236).

Khoresht-e Alū
Lamb and Dried Plum Stew

My paternal grandmother, who we simply called "The Lady," was a fabulous cook and storyteller. She had beautiful sky-blue eyes and pitch-black hair and spoke very little Farsi (the language I grew up speaking). I often stayed with my grandparents for long stretches of time as a child. The Lady would spoil me with treats and tell me amazing fables and stories of princes and princesses in Turki (a language akin to Turkish spoken in many parts of Iran) while I watched her cook. Her lamb and dried plum stew was a particular favorite of mine. This is my long-gone blue-eyed grandmother's recipe.

SERVES 4–6

4 tablespoons oil, plus more for frying

2 onions, finely chopped

14 oz (400 g) boneless lamb neck fillet or lean shoulder, cut into chunks

1¼ teaspoons ground turmeric

½ teaspoon mild curry powder

2 tablespoons tomato paste

12 Persian golden plums (ālū bokhārā) or 8 dried apricots

2 medium russet or similar potatoes, cubed

1½ tablespoons salt

½ cup (3½ oz/100 g) Persian yellow lentils (or use chana dal; see glossary entry for lapeh, page 306)

8 pitted prunes

Parsley leaves, to garnish (optional)

Heat 2 tablespoons of the oil in a heavy pot or Dutch oven over medium heat and lightly brown the onions. Add the meat, turmeric, and curry powder and fry until the meat is browned on all sides. Add the tomato paste and cook for 2 minutes. Pour over enough boiling water to cover the meat by a fingertip. Bring to a boil, then lower the heat, cover, and braise gently for 1½ hours or until the meat is just tender.

While the meat is cooking, cover the golden plums or apricots with cold water and allow to soak for about 30 minutes or until plump. Place the cubed potatoes in a bowlful of cold water, add the salt, and set aside.

Put the yellow lentils or chana dal in a small saucepan and cover with water. Bring to a gentle simmer and cook until the lentils are soft but still firm in the center (check package instructions; cooking times vary). Rinse with cold water and set aside.

When the meat is almost tender, drain the plums or apricots and add them to the stew, along with the prunes and lentils. Add a little boiling water if the meat juices aren't enough to cover all the ingredients. Bring to a gentle boil, lower the heat, and continue to cook until the lentils are tender but not mushy. Remove from the heat as soon as the lentils are cooked through.

Twenty minutes before serving, fry the potato cubes according to the instructions for sīb zamīnī sorkh kardeh (page 281). Reheat the stew and stir in half of the fried potatoes. Cook for a few minutes and garnish with the rest of the potatoes and the parsley (if using). Serve with chelō (page 236) or kateh (page 239).

Morgh-e Lavangī
Stuffed Poussin with Plums and Walnuts

I first ate this dish in Talesh, a very lush, green region to the west of the Caspian Sea where the local people make it for special occasions. The pesto-like stuffing, called lavangī, is made with walnuts and plum paste. In Talesh, wild sour plums or tart wild medlars grow abundantly in the region's dense forests, but they are hard to come by elsewhere. I make my own plum paste with regular plums from the supermarket and freeze it in ice cube trays to use whenever needed. Plum paste is superb added to stews to give a malas (sweet and sour) flavor or when used as a stuffing, combined with other ingredients, as in this recipe.

SERVES 4

6 large tart plums, preferably red

½ teaspoon cinnamon

½ teaspoon ground black pepper

½ teaspoon sea salt

1¾ cups (5 oz/150 g) ground walnuts

1 small onion, grated

3 tablespoons oil

2 poussins (or use 1 whole chicken)

3 large tomatoes, quartered

Salt and black pepper

1 tablespoon slivered pistachios or chopped parsley or cilantro, to garnish

Pit and chop the plums and put them in a small saucepan with a few tablespoons of water and a large pinch of salt. Cook until the fruit is falling apart. Push the pulp through a seive and return to the pot. Reduce over high heat until a thick paste is formed. Reserve 2 tablespoons of the paste for later, then mix the rest with the cinnamon, black pepper, the reamaining salt, and the ground walnuts. Fry the onion with 1 tablespoon of the oil until lightly golden, then add to the plum and walnut mixture.

Using the tips of your fingers, release the skin from the breasts of the poussins and rub some of the stuffing onto the meat. Be careful not to tear the skin. Use the rest of the mixture to stuff the cavity, then tie the legs with string to secure the filling.

Preheat the oven to 350°F (180°C). Heat the remaining oil in a large Dutch oven over medium heat and brown the poussins on all sides. Brush with the reserved plum paste. Add the quartered tomatoes to the dish and season with salt and pepper.

Tightly cover the pot and bake for 1 hour (if you're using chicken, it will need around 2 hours, depending on weight). Baste the poussins then bake, uncovered, for a further 15 minutes or until the skin is golden, basting the birds a couple more times. Garnish with slivered pistachios or chopped herbs and serve with chelō (page 236) or kateh (page 239).

Khoresht-e Porteghāl
Chicken in Orange and Saffron Sauce

This dish hails from the region around the Caspian Sea where oranges, clementines, grapefruits, lemons, and kumquats are grown in abundance. This dish used to be virtually unknown in most other parts of the country until its popularity began to grow through television cooking shows over the last few years. I love to use slightly sour new season oranges for a bit of tang and added depth of flavor. Balance out the sourness with sugar, tasting as you go.

SERVES 4

3 small oranges

2 tablespoons oil

4 chicken legs

2 tablespoons (1 oz/30 g) butter

1 red onion, finely chopped

1 teaspoon ground turmeric

½ tablespoon tomato paste

2½ cups (600 ml) fresh orange juice

A small piece of cinnamon (about ⅓ inch/1 cm)

¼ teaspoon ground white pepper (optional)

½ teaspoon saffron water (page 278)

½ teaspoon salt

Juice of one small lemon

Sugar, to taste

A few cilantro or flat-leaf parsley leaves, to garnish

Remove the top and bottom of each orange so they stand upright, then use a sharp knife to peel them in strips, reserving the peel of 1 orange. Cut the peeled oranges into thick slices. Remove the pith from the reserved peel and slice it thinly.

Heat the oil in a large lidded frying pan over medium heat and fry the chicken until golden on all sides. Remove from the pan and set aside. Add the butter to the frying pan and fry the onions until golden. Sprinkle over the turmeric and fry for 2 minutes. Add the tomato paste, orange juice, cinnamon, white pepper, sliced peel, saffron water, and salt and stir. Place the chicken in the sauce, cover, and bring to a boil. Simmer for 45 minutes, until the chicken pieces are well cooked and the sauce has reduced by two-thirds.

Arrange the orange slices over the chicken and add any juice to the pan. Add the lemon juice and a pinch of sugar (to taste) to balance the flavors. Taste and adjust the seasoning to your liking. Cook gently for a few minutes to soften the fruit, basting the oranges with the sauce from time to time. Garnish with cilantro or parsley and serve with chelōh (page 236) or kateh (page 239).

Mūtanjan
Duck in Walnut Sauce

This lavish dish from Gilan is often prepared with duck for banquets and chicken for more everyday occasions. The bird is cooked slowly in its rich fruity sauce until the meat is falling off the bone and the sauce is thick. A layer of delicious oil on top, released from the walnuts, is a sign the dish is ready. As with any stew flavored with pomegranate molasses, the quantity given in the recipe is just for guidance. Different brands vary hugely in thickness and flavor so add the molasses gradually.

SERVES 4

3 tablespoons oil

4 duck legs

1 onion, finely chopped

1 teaspoon ground turmeric

2 tablespoons tomato paste

2½ cups (7 oz/200 g) ground walnuts

2 cups (500 ml) hot water

1 teaspoon salt

½ teaspoon cinnamon

½ teaspoon black pepper

Generous ¾ cup (200 ml) pomegranate molasses, or to taste

1½ cups (7 oz/200 g) dried apricots

⅓ cup (2 oz/60 g) green or black raisins

Pinch of sugar (optional)

A few chopped pistachios, to garnish

Heat 1 tablespoon of the oil in a large Dutch oven and fry the duck legs until well browned on all sides. Remove from the pan and set aside.

Add the onion to the pan with another tablespoon of the oil. Cook, stirring from time to time, until golden, then add the turmeric and tomato paste. Stir and cook for 2 minutes. Add the ground walnuts to the pan and cook for 3–4 minutes, stirring all the time. Add the hot water, salt, cinnamon, and black pepper and stir well. Bring to a gentle boil, then lower the heat and add the duck legs, along with any juices. Cover and simmer gently over low heat for 2 hours, or until the meat is very tender. Stir from time to time so it doesn't catch on the bottom. If the water is evaporating too quickly add a few ice cubes, which will also help release the oils from the walnuts. Gradually add the pomegranate molasses and stir well. Simmer for 30 minutes.

Heat the remaining 1 tablespoon oil in a small frying pan over medium heat and lightly sauté the apricots and raisins. Reserve an apricot and a few raisins to garnish and add the rest to the sauce. Continue to simmer very gently over very low heat until the duck is falling off the bone, 20–30 minutes.

Taste and add more pomegranate molasses and salt if required. You can also add a pinch of sugar to balance the flavor. Chop the reserved apricot. Garnish the dish with the reserved raisins, apricot, and pistachios and serve with chelō (page 236) or rice with noodles (page 205).

Dolmeh-ye Beh
Sweet and Sour Stuffed Quinces

Quinces have been cultivated in Iran since ancient times and the fruit has always been highly regarded both for its culinary uses and medicinal properties. Their trees have gorgeous fragrant blossoms in spring, and beautiful dawn-yellow fruit in autumn. This elegant dish from the western province of Oroumiyeh is exotic even by Iranian standards, and takes a bit of skill and effort to make. It will keep very well for a couple of days in the fridge, so is a perfect make-ahead dish for dinner parties.

SERVES 4

16 Persian dried golden plums (ālū bokhārā) or prunes

Scant ½ cup (3 oz/80 g) Persian yellow lentils (or use chana dal; see glossary entry for lapeh, page 306)

3 tablespoons (1½ oz/40 g) butter

1 onion, chopped

10½ oz (300 g) lean ground beef

½ teaspoon black pepper

1 teaspoon ground turmeric

¼ teaspoon cinnamon

¼ teaspoon ground coriander

¼ teaspoon ground cumin

¾ teaspoon salt

1¾ cups (400 ml) boiling water

¼ teaspoon saffron water (page 278)

4 large quinces

Fresh lemon juice, to taste

Sugar, to taste

1 teaspoon slivered or chopped pistachios

Put the plums or prunes in a small bowl and cover with water to soak while you are prepare the other ingredients. Place the lentils in a small saucepan and cover with water. Bring to a boil, then lower the heat and cook until tender. Drain in a sieve and rinse well.

Melt the butter in a deep frying pan and sauté the onions until golden. Remove half and set aside. Add the meat, pepper, and ½ teaspoon of the turmeric, and brown the meat. Add the cinnamon, coriander, cumin, and salt and cook for another few minutes. Turn off the heat and stir in the rinsed lentils.

Put the reserved onions into a large heavy-bottomed pot that can fit all the quinces. Sprinkle over the remaining turmeric and cook over medium heat for a minute or two. Pour in the boiling water and the saffron water and bring to a gentle simmer.

Peel the quinces and cut a thick slice from the top of each to use as a lid. Hollow out the quinces, leaving a shell about ½ inch (1½ cm) thick. Chop the flesh and add it to the meat. Stuff the quinces with the meat mixture and top with the reserved lids. Place them in the sauce, and add the soaked plums or prunes. Cover and simmer gently for 1½ hours, basting from time to time, until the quinces are soft.

Taste and adjust the sweet and sour flavor to your liking with lemon juice and sugar, starting with ½ teaspoon of each. Simmer, uncovered, until the sauce has reduced to a thin gravy. Sprinkle over the pistachios and serve.

Holū Kabāb
Sweet and Sour Stuffed Meatballs

Holū means peach in Farsi, but the sweet and sour sauce in which these meatballs are cooked doesn't call for any. My guess is these were originally made as round and big as peaches, hence the odd-seeming name. This is a good make-ahead dish because it keeps well in the fridge and taste even better after a couple of days.

SERVES 4

Scant ½ cup (3 oz/80 g) Persian yellow lentils (or use chana dal; see glossary entry for lapeh, page 306)

1 medium potato

1 onion, chopped

4 tablespoons oil

1 teaspoon ground turmeric

3 tablespoons currants

9 oz (250 g) lean ground beef

1 egg

½ teaspoon ground black pepper

½ teaspoon salt

½ teaspoon cinnamon

3 tablespoons coarsely chopped walnuts

½ cup (120 ml) fresh lemon juice

½ cup (120 ml) water

¼ cup (1¾ oz/50 g) sugar

1 tablespoon tomato paste

½ teaspoon saffron water (page 278)

Walnut halves and chives, to garnish (optional)

Put the lentils in a small saucepan and cover with cold water. Bring to a gentle boil. Lower the heat and cook uncovered until soft. Drain in a sieve and rinse with cold water. Set aside.

Parboil the unpeeled potato and allow it to cool, then cut it into chunks. In a large frying pan, fry the onion with 1 tablespoon of the oil and ½ teaspoon of the turmeric until golden brown. Remove from the pan and set aside.

Sauté the currants with another tablespoon of the oil for a minute or two on low heat or until they are just heated through and shiny. Remove and set aside.

Put the meat, potato, lentils, egg, pepper, salt, cinnamon, and the rest of the turmeric in a food processor and process until well mixed and dough-like. Divide the mixture into four. Oil your hands lightly and shape each portion into an ovoid in the palm of your hand. Put some of the fried onions, a few currants, and a couple of walnut pieces in the middle, and bring the sides over the stuffing to completely cover. Neaten the shape and set on a plate. Shape and stuff the rest of the mixture, reserving a few currants to use as a garnish.

Heat the remaining oil in the frying pan over medium heat and fry the meatballs until lightly golden all over.

Mix the lemon juice, water, sugar, tomato paste, a pinch of salt, and the saffron water, and pour onto the meatballs. Cover and simmer over low heat for 30–45 minutes, turning a few times. You may need to add some boiling water if the sauce is evaporating too fast. Garnish with the remaining currants and the walnut halves and chives, and serve warm or at room temperature.

Kūfteh Berenjī
Herbed Meatballs

The Farsi word kūfteh, meaning meatball, has made its way into many languages including South Asian, Armenian, Turkish, Bulgarian, Greek, Slovenian, and Arabic. The wide geographical distribution of the word (as kofta, kefteh, köfte, etc.) marks the spread of Persian food and culture throughout the ancient world and its legacy in many modern world cuisines. Persian kūftehs are always cooked in a broth or sauce, never baked or deep-fried. The broth may be eaten like a soup, with torn flatbread soaked into it. The following recipe is quite a common one. You can use fresh herbs if you wish but the dried kind make shaping the kūfteh much easier.

SERVES 4

3 tablespoons oil, plus more if needed

1½ tablespoons (¾ oz/20 g) butter

1 onion, finely chopped

1 teaspoon ground turmeric

1 tablespoon tomato paste

Salt

8 cups (2 liters) boiling water

Handful of barberries, to garnish

FOR THE MEATBALLS

9 oz (250 g) ground beef or lamb

1 onion, coarsely chopped

½ teaspoon ground turmeric

½ teaspoon ground black pepper

½ teaspoon ground cumin

½ teaspoon ground coriander

2 tablespoons dried mint

1 tablespoon dried tarragon

1 tablespoon dried dill

1 egg

2 tablespoons chickpea flour

Scant ½ cup (2½ oz/70 g) Thai jasmine or Arborio rice, parboiled

¼ cup (1¾ oz/50 g) Persian yellow lentils or chana dal, parboiled

10 dried Persian plums or dried apricots (optional)

First make the sauce: put the oil and butter in a large pan and cook the onion until golden. Add the turmeric and tomato paste and cook for 2 minutes. Add ½ teaspoon salt and the boiling water and return to a boil. Lower the heat and simmer very gently.

For the meatballs, combine the meat, onion, spices, herbs, egg, chickpea flour, and 1 teaspoon salt in a food processor and process until the mixture is doughy. Stir in the parboiled rice and lentils and knead well by hand. Divide the mixture into four and, with wet hands, shape each into an even ball.

Drop a meatball into the simmering sauce and wait for it to come back to a gentle simmer again before adding the next one. With a large spoon, roll the meatballs in the broth, which must almost cover them. Add some more hot water if required, then add the plums or apricots, if using. Cover the saucepan and allow the kūfteh to simmer gently over low heat for 1 hour, or until the plums are cooked and the sauce has reduced to your liking. Taste and adjust the seasoning.

Heat a small splash of oil in a small saucepan and cook the barberries, stirring, over very low heat for 1 minute or until shiny and puffed up. Use this to garnish the meatballs.

Serve with flatbread, sabzī khordan (page 98), and a torshī of your choice (pages 262–271).

Dolmeh Bādemjūn

Stuffed Vegetables

Every country in the Middle East has its own version of stuffed vegetables. Eggplants, zucchini, peppers, tomatoes, and onions are commonly used, though you can stuff most things—my grandma used to stuff unripe melons at the end of the season when there was no hope they would ripen. This recipe is from Tabriz, my parents' hometown, and uses warming spices such as cinnamon and allspice to give it a suitably autumnal flavor. My grandma always made this with long, slender eggplants, but the chubby rounded Italian ones are much easier to hollow out.

SERVES 4

4 tablespoons oil

2 onions, finely chopped

7 oz (200 g) boneless lamb neck fillet or lean shoulder, cut into small cubes

½ teaspoon ground black pepper

¼ teaspoon ground cumin

¼ teaspoon ground coriander

¼ teaspoon cinnamon

¼ teaspoon allspice

1 teaspoon ground turmeric

1 teaspoon salt

3 tablespoons tomato paste

Generous ¾ cup (5 oz/150 g) Thai jasmine rice

Boiling water

¾ cup (5 oz/150 g) Persian yellow lentils (or use chana dal; see glossary entry for lapeh, page 306)

3 small fat eggplants

2 medium tomatoes

2 red peppers

A handful of herbs, to garnish

Drizzle 2 tablespoons of the oil in a lidded frying pan and sauté the onions until golden. Remove half for the sauce, and add the lamb to the rest. Cook over medium heat until the lamb is lightly browned all over. Add the spices, salt, and tomato paste and cook for 2 minutes, stirring. Add a scant ½ cup (100 ml) water and bring to a boil. Cover and cook for 30–45 minutes over low heat until the lamb is soft and the water has evaporated. Transfer to a bowl.

Meanwhile, put the rice in a small saucepan and fill with water. Swirl the rice around and drain. Add 1¾ cups (400 ml) boiling water and bring back to a boil. Cook the rice until just al dente. Drain and set aside. Wash and drain the lentils and boil until soft but not mushy. Drain and rinse. Set aside.

Cut off the leaf-like tips of the green cap covering the top of the eggplant, but keep the stem attached. Cut about ½ inch (1½ cm) below the cap and keep to use as a lid. Put each eggplant on a chopping board and roll to soften the flesh. Use a small spoon to scoop out as much flesh from the inside as you can, leaving a shell just under ½ inch (1 cm) thick. Discard the pulp (or sauté and use in another dish). Cut a slice from the top of the tomatoes and scoop out the flesh with a small spoon, leaving a shell just under ½ inch (1 cm) thick. Cut the top off the peppers, and remove the seeds and membranes.

Heat the remaining oil in a heavy pot or Dutch oven large enough to hold all of the eggplants and tomatoes. Fry the eggplant shells over medium-low heat with the lid on, turning

occasionally so they brown a little all over. Lift from the pan and set aside.

Put the reserved onions in the pot with a pinch of salt and cook over medium heat for 2 minutes. Add 1 cup (250 ml) boiling water and bring to a boil. Lower the heat and leave to simmer while you stuff the vegetables.

Combine the cooked rice and yellow lentils with the lamb and fill the vegetables almost to the top. Put the eggplant caps back on and secure with toothpicks. Cover the tomatoes and peppers with their lids. Carefully place the eggplants in the sauce and arrange the tomatoes around them.

Spoon some sauce over the vegetables. Cover and simmer very gently for 30 minutes or until the sauce is reduced by half. Alternatively, cover loosely with foil and bake in an oven preheated to 350°F (180°C) for 30–45 minutes, removing the foil for the last 10 minutes. Remove the toothpicks and garnish with a handful of herbs. Serve warm or cold with sabzī khordan (page 98), plenty of yogurt, and flatbread.

Kalam Ghomrī Polō
Saffron Rice with Kohlrabi and Meatballs

I get excited whenever I find kohlrabi in farmers' markets or our local Turkish food shop. This incredibly tasty but underrated vegetable from the cabbage family is grown for its globe-like root rather than the leaves. In this polō, the sugars in the kohlrabi caramelize and impart a sweet flavor to the delicately spiced rice. I prefer a sliced potato tahdīg for this dish, but feel free to line the base with flatbread or make it with plain rice (according to the instructions on page 236). For a vegetarian version use sautéed mushrooms in place of the meatballs.

SERVES 4–6

2 cups (14 oz/400 g) white long grain rice

1 lb (500 g) kohlrabi, peeled and diced

4 tablespoons oil

1 teaspoon ground turmeric

1 teaspoon cumin seeds

½ teaspoon ground black pepper

½ teaspoon smoked sea salt flakes

Salt

1 quantity tiny meatballs (page 282)

2 baking potatoes, thickly sliced

1½ tablespoons (¾ oz/20 g) butter

2 teaspoons saffron water (page 278)

Wash and soak the rice according to the instructions for chelō (page 236). Sauté the diced kohlrabi with 2 tablespoons of the oil in a frying pan over medium heat until it begins to turn a little brown at the edges. Add the turmeric, cumin, pepper, and smoked salt and continue to cook for 2 minutes. Remove from the pan and set aside.

Prepare and cook the meatballs according to the instructions on page 282. Boil the rice and drain according to the instructions for chelō. Pour the remaining 2 tablespoons oil into a saucepan, preferably nonstick, and place over medium heat. When the oil is sizzling, sprinkle over a little salt and arrange the potato slices in the bottom of the pot. Cover with one-third of the rice, then half of the kohlrabi and half of the meatballs. Repeat until all the ingredients are used up. Shape the rice into a mound so it doesn't touch the sides of the saucepan. Cover with a lid wrapped in a dish towel and heat over medium-low heat until the side of the saucepan sizzles when touched with a wet finger.

Meanwhile, melt the butter with 2 tablespoons of water and pour over the rice. Cover again and reduce the heat to very low. Steam for 30–45 minutes, until the rice is tender.

Mix the saffron water with some of the plain rice. Transfer the rest of the rice to a platter and cover with the saffron rice. Arrange the potato slices around the rice. Serve immediately with torshī (page 262–271) and sabzī khordan (page 98).

Polō bā Kadū Halvāī

Jeweled Butternut Squash Rice

This is a common dish in Mazandaran province, just to the south of the Caspian Sea, where it can be a humble everyday meal eaten with fried eggs, or a much more elaborate one garnished with almonds, pistachios, and barberries and served with saffron-braised chicken, or layered with tiny fried meatballs before steaming. The best tahdīg for this dish is just plain rice, but if you are feeling adventurous you could try putting a few thick slices of squash in the bottom of the pan. Squash burns fast so use a heat diffuser, turn the heat down as low as you can, and keep an eye on it.

SERVES 4–6

2 cups (14 oz/400 g) white long grain rice

3 tablespoons (1½ oz/40 g) butter

1 medium butternut squash, cut into small cubes

Pinch of salt

¼ teaspoon cinnamon

¾ teaspoon cumin seeds, or ½ teaspoon ground cumin

1 tablespoon light brown sugar

1 tablespoon slivered almonds

1 tablespoon slivered pistachios

1½ tablespoons barberries

1 tablespoon oil

1 quantity tiny meatballs (page 282), or fried eggs, to serve

Wash and soak the rice according to the instructions for chelō (page 236). Use about one-quarter of the butter to fry the squash cubes over medium heat until lightly caramelized. Sprinkle with a pinch of salt and the spices and sauté until fragrant—about 2 minutes. Add the sugar and stir gently to coat the cubes. Remove the squash from the pan and set aside.

Sauté the nuts and barberries with another quarter of the butter for 1 minute, or until the barberries puff up a little. Return the squash to the pan and stir gently to mix the ingredients. Turn off the heat.

Boil the rice according to the instructions for chelō. Drain in a colander or sieve. Heat the oil in a pot over medium heat. Cover with one-third of the rice, then half of the squash mixture, and half of the tiny meatballs, if using. Repeat until all the rice and squash is used up. Cover with the lid (wrapped in a clean dish towel) right away to keep the steam in the pot. When the side of the pot sizzles when touched with a wet finger, melt the remaining butter with 1 tablespoon of water and drizzle evenly over the rice. Cover again, and steam the rice over very low heat for 20–30 minutes, or until there is a lot of steam when you lift the lid and the rice in the bottom of the pan has turned golden and crisp. Serve immediately with the rest of the tiny meatballs or some fried eggs. Serve with sālād shīrāzī (page 250).

Tahchīn-e Esfenaj
Saffron Rice Cake with Lamb and Spinach

The gorgeous golden, green, and white layers of this savory rice cake hide chunks of succulent lamb. It may look like it takes a lot of effort to make but it's quite simple. Tahchīn with lamb and spinach is a speciality of the northern Mazandaran region where the spinach layer is sometimes mixed with pomegranate molasses. I prefer to add a little dried lime powder to the spinach, as in the following recipe. If you don't have this, just add a little fresh lemon juice instead.

SERVES 4–6

2 cups (14 oz/400 g) white long grain rice

6 tablespoons oil

2 onions, thinly sliced

14 oz (400 g) boneless lamb shoulder, leg, or neck fillet, cut into thick medallions

¼ teaspoon ground turmeric

½ teaspoon salt

½ tablespoon black peppercorns

1 bay leaf

2 cloves of garlic

1 lb (500 g) baby spinach

Salt and black pepper

3 tablespoons Greek yogurt, lightly beaten

1 tablespoon fresh lemon juice

2 egg yolks

1½ teaspoons saffron water (page 278)

1 teaspoon dried lime powder (optional)

1 tablespoon (½ oz/15 g) butter, melted

Herbs or spinach leaves, to garnish

Wash and soak the rice according to the instructions for chelō (page 236). Put 2 tablespoons of the oil in a medium saucepan and gently fry the onions until golden. Remove half of the onions and set aside. Increase the heat to high and add the lamb to the onions in the pan. Cook until browned. Sprinkle over the turmeric and cook for 1 minute. Add the ½ teaspoon of salt, peppercorns, bay leaf, garlic, and 1¼ cups (300 ml) water. Cover and cook over very low heat for 1½ hours or until the lamb is meltingly tender.

Put the reserved onions in a large deep frying pan. Add the spinach and 1 tablespoon water. Cover and cook over medium-low heat for a few minutes to wilt the spinach. Season with salt and pepper. Stir and cook, uncovered, for 5 minutes.

Remove the lamb from its broth and set aside. Discard the bay leaf, peppercorns, and garlic cloves. Add the broth to the spinach and cook off until the spinach is almost dry. Set aside.

Whisk together the yogurt, 2 tablespoons of the oil, the lemon juice, egg yolks, and saffron water. Boil the rice according to the instructions for chelō and drain when al dente. Rinse, then stir one-third of the rice into the yogurt mixture.

Preheat the oven to 400°F (200°C). Heat the remaining 2 tablespoons oil in a 10 inch (25 cm) Dutch oven or nonstick ovensafe pot for 4 minutes, or until a few rice grains thrown in the oil sizzle. When the oil is very hot, pour in the yogurt and rice mixture and level the surface. Arrange the lamb over the

rice, sprinkle with the dried lime powder (if using) and cover with the spinach mixture. Top with the plain rice, level the surface, and pour the melted butter over evenly. Cover tightly with foil.

Bake in the oven for 1½–2 hours or until you can see a golden crust around the edge. If you don't want to cook it immediately, you can leave the tahchīn in the fridge for a few hours or even overnight. Just make sure to allow it to come to room temperature for an hour before baking.

Remove the pot from the oven. Put a large plate over the pot and, holding firmly with both hands, flip the pot and the plate together. Garnish the rice cake with herbs or baby spinach leaves and serve immediately with sabzī khordan (page 98) and sālād shīrāzī (page 250).

Zereshk Polō

Rice with Barberries

I can say without a shred of doubt that zereshk polō is a favorite of every Iranian. All Persian restaurants serves this rice and it is almost always on the menu at weddings, birthdays, and funerals. If you are making this for a special occasion you can indulge yourself by adding slivered pistachio nuts and blanched almonds to the barberries as Persian cooks often do to create a kaleidoscope of color. I sometimes make my zereshk polō with saffron tahdīg (page 230), which makes the dish even more special, but flatbread or potatoes work very nicely too. We eat zereshk polō with chicken. Braised chicken in tomato sauce (page 243) and braised saffron chicken (page 240) are both perfect partners for this dish.

SERVES 4-6

1 quantity chelō (page 236)

Your preferred tahdīg ingredients (see page 230)

⅓ cup (1¾ oz/50 g) barberries

2 teaspoons butter

1 teaspoon saffron water (page 278)

A few slivered pistachios, to garnish (optional)

Wash, soak, boil, and steam the rice according to the instructions for chelō (page 236), with your preferred kind of tahdīg (see page 230).

While you are waiting for the rice to cook, pick over the barberries and put them in a small bowl. Cover with water. Swirl around a few times and drain well. Set aside.

A few minutes before serving, melt the butter in a small saucepan. Add the barberries and swirl around for a couple of minutes or until they are puffed up.

When the rice is done, place a few heaped tablespoons in a small bowl and mix with the saffron. Transfer half of the remaining rice to a platter. Cover with one-half of the barberries and one-half of the saffron rice. Repeat with the rest of the plain rice, the remaining saffron rice, and the rest of the barberries. Sprinkle a few slivered pistachios on top. You can pour more melted butter on top if you wish.

Take out the crispy rice (or other tahdīg) from the bottom of the pot. Break into small pieces and serve with the rice.

Yatīmcheh
Slow-Cooked Vegetable Stew

This is my ultimate all-vegetable comfort food. I can't tell you how delicious it is, in spite of its slightly off-putting Persian name, which translates as "orphan's stew." It's important to cook this long and slow to allow the flavors to meld together—I sometimes leave this on the smallest burner of my stove for as long as three hours. Serve this with any kind of bread you like and a bowl of yogurt on the side, or spooned over rice. Leftovers are even more delicious the next day.

SERVES 4

8 tablespoons oil

2 medium eggplants, thickly sliced

8 very small red onions

1 teaspoon ground turmeric

1 teaspoon salt

½ teaspoon ground black pepper

¼ teaspoon cayenne pepper (optional)

½ teaspoon dried lime powder (optional)

4 cloves of garlic, thinly sliced

1 large red pepper, cut into pieces

4 tomatoes, thickly sliced

2 potatoes, peeled and thickly sliced

Drizzle 2½ tablespoons of the oil into a medium nonstick pan and arrange half the sliced eggplants in the pot. Cover with a lid and cook over medium heat for 5 minutes or until they are golden brown on the bottom. Turn the slices over and fry the other side without adding more oil or covering. Remove from the pan and repeat with the rest of the slices, adding another 2½ tablespoons oil to the pan. Set aside.

Finely chop two of the onions. Add 2 tablespoons oil to the saucepan and cook the chopped onions over medium heat for 10 minutes or until golden brown. Add the turmeric and cook for 1 minute. Remove from the pan and set aside. In a small bowl, mix the salt, pepper, cayenne, and dried lime powder.

Put the remaining 1 tablespoon oil in the pan. Thickly slice the remaining onions and arrange them in the bottom of the pan. Cover with the fried eggplant, then sprinkle with one-third of the spice mix, half of the fried onions, and half of the sliced garlic. Add the red pepper, the rest of the garlic, and the rest of the fried onions. Cover with the tomato slices and sprinkle with the rest of the spices. Arrange the potato slices over the top and cover the pan. Cook over medium heat on the medium burner of your stovetop for 3 minutes, then turn down the heat to low and cook for at least 1 hour or until the sauce has reduced to a few tablespoons. If the sauce is evaporating too fast, turn down the heat or add 1 tablespoon water from the kettle. Serve warm or at room temperature with bread or rice.

Nūn-e Zanjafīlī-ye Tabrīz
Savory Ginger Loaves

Ginger loaves are a speciality of Tabrīz where my parents come from. My mom used to bake huge batches for breakfast, but I never made them myself until I left Iran and started having cravings for them. We eat these spicy loaves smeared with lots of butter and creamy white cheese with strong sweetened black tea to wash them down. I keep them in the freezer in airtight bags and just warm one in the oven while I'm making tea and setting out the butter and cheese.

MAKES 8 LOAVES

4 cups (1 lb/500 g) all-purpose flour

1 tablespoon instant yeast

3 tablespoons ground ginger

1½ teaspoons sea salt, crushed

1 egg, lightly beaten

½ cup (120 ml) vegetable oil, plus more for oiling

Generous ¾ cup (200 ml) luke-warm water

Generous ¾ cup (200 ml) plain yogurt, at room temperature

Very small pinch of ground saffron

1 tablespoon boiling water

1 egg yolk, lightly beaten

Walnut halves, to decorate

½ teaspoon nigella seeds, to decorate (optional)

Preheat the oven to 425°F (220°C). Line a baking sheet with parchment paper and oil lightly.

Put half of the flour in a bowl with the yeast, ginger, and salt and mix well. In a separate bowl, mix the egg, oil, water, and yogurt. Make a well in the center of the flour and add the wet ingredients mixture. Mix with a wooden spoon, then gradually add the rest of the flour, using your hand to mix as you go. Stop adding flour once the dough is elastic and no longer sticks to your hands.

Place the dough on a floured surface and knead for 10 minutes. Put in a lightly oiled bowl and cover. Leave in a warm place until doubled in size—about 2 hours.

Combine the saffron with the 1 tablespoon boiling water. Leave to cool before adding the egg yolk. Mix well and set aside.

Punch down the dough and divide into eight pieces. Shape each piece into a round loaf, around ½ inch (1 cm) thick. Cover with a dish towel and leave to rest for 20 minutes.

Use a small round cookie cutter to create shapes on the top of the loaves. Decorate with the walnut halves, brush generously with the saffron egg wash, and sprinkle over some nigella seeds, if using. Bake for 25–30 minutes or until golden brown.

Halvā-ye Beh
Quince Halva

In Farsi, any sweet paste is called halvā (from the Arabic, meaning sweet). The most common halvā is made with flour, saffron, and rosewater. Other varieties include carrot halvā, sesame seed halvā, walnut halvā, and rose petal halvā (page 227). This rather rare quince halvā hails from Gilan in northern Iran and is made without any flour or oil. Unlike other types of halvā, this has a lovely sweet and sour flavor. It is usually cut into small diamonds or squares and is eaten like a sweetmeat with tea.

MAKES 15-20 PIECES
2–3 large quinces
Squeeze of lemon juice
2½ cups (1 lb/500 g) sugar, or as needed
¼ teaspoon coarsely ground cardamom seeds (optional)
A small handful of lightly toasted slivered almonds, chopped pistachios or walnuts (optional)

Peel, core, and thinly slice the quinces, dropping them in a bowl of water with a squeeze of lemon juice as you go to prevent them turning brown. Drain the slices and place in a heavy-bottomed pot. Add ½ cup (3½ oz/100 g) of the sugar and enough water to cover. Cover and cook over low heat for about 1½ hours or until the fruit is soft and all the water has been absorbed.

Mash the quince pulp, then measure the pulp with a cup. For every cup of quince add 1 cup of sugar and stir well. You may need slightly more or less than the amount given in the ingredients list, depending on how much pulp your quinces yield. Cook the sweetened pulp over medium heat, stirring constantly, until you have a thick paste that forms a loose ball in the center of the pan. Stir in the cardamom and/or nuts, if using, and turn off the heat.

Line a small round or square dish with plastic wrap. Turn the quince paste into the dish and smooth over with a spoon. Cover and allow to set for at least half a day. You don't need to refrigerate it at this stage, but once it's set you can keep it in the fridge for several weeks. To serve, cut into squares or diamonds.

Komāj-e Beh
Stuffed Quinces in Pastry

I have vivid memories of the fruit room in my grandparents' house in Tabriz, where huge bunches of grapes hung from the ceiling and wooden boxes filled with quinces lined the walls. The quinces were wrapped in thick layers of cotton in order to keep these seasonal delicacies intact until spring. When I found this long-forgotten recipe in the sixteenth-century *Manual on Cooking and its Craft*, I just had to try it. The recipe called for four quinces to be stuffed then placed in a deep dish lined with pastry, with another layer of pastry on top to seal them in. Though I experimented with various pastries and cooking methods, these individually wrapped quinces were by far the best. These delicious little pies are excellent made with apples too.

SERVES 1–2

3½ tablespoons ground pistachios

⅓ cup (1 oz/30 g) ground almonds

⅔ cup (3 oz/80 g) confectioner's sugar

Heaped ¼ teaspoon cardamom

½ teaspoon cinnamon

½–1 teaspoon rosewater, to taste

1 large quince or large cooking apple

1 sheet ready-made pie crust pastry sheets

1 egg yolk

A few drops of saffron water (page 278, optional)

Preheat the oven to 400°F (200°C). Mix together the ground nuts, confectioner's sugar, cardamom, cinnamon, and rosewater. Cut a big slice from the top of the quince or apple and reserve to use as a lid. Hollow out the fruit, leaving a ¾ inch (2 cm) thick shell. Be careful not to break the shell. Finely chop the pulp and add it to the nut mixture. Peel the quince and pack it tightly with the stuffing. Put the lid back on.

Put the quince on the sheet of pastry and cut around it to make a base. Drape the remaining pastry over the quince so it is completely covered, and trim off any excess. Work with your hands to shape the pastry over the fruit and press the two pieces together. Remove any extra pastry with a sharp knife. Use the excess to cut out leaves to decorate if you like.

Mix the egg yolk with a few drops of saffron water (if using) and 1½ teaspoons water and lightly beat. Brush this over the pastry then carefully place on a baking sheet. Bake for 30 minutes on the middle rack of the oven, then reduce the heat to 350°F (180°C) and bake for a further 15–20 minutes or until the pastry is golden. Remove from the oven and allow to cool before cutting into wedges and serving with hot tea.

Kākā

Butternut Squash Pancakes

These lightly spiced pancakes are traditionally made with homemade rice flour in the northern regions of Iran, where rice farmers grow a few squash plants in their vegetable patches. Their squash look and taste like butternut squash, but are huge, weighing several pounds each. These pancakes are delicious on their own or with a sprinkling of confectioner's sugar, but I love to eat them with butternut squash preserve (page 284) and its delicious syrup. The pancakes keep well for a few days in an airtight dish.

SERVES 4

7 oz (200 g) butternut squash, peeled and diced

¼ cup (1½ oz/40 g) rice flour

2 tablespoons ground walnuts

¼ teaspoon cardamom

½ teaspoon cinnamon

Pinch of ground ginger

¼ teaspoon baking soda

Pinch of salt

1½ tablespoons sugar

1 tablespoon yogurt

½ tablespoon rosewater (optional)

1 large egg

1 tablespoon oil

Butter, for frying and to serve

Maple syrup or butternut squash preserve (page 284), to serve

Chopped walnutes, to serve (optional)

Put the squash in a small saucepan and add 2–3 tablespoons water. Cover and cook over low heat until very soft and most of the water has evaporated. Mash with a fork or potato masher.

Mix together the rice flour, ground walnuts, spices, baking soda, salt, and sugar. In a separate bowl, whisk the yogurt, rosewater, egg, and oil and pour over the dry ingredients. Stir well, then mix with the squash and leave to stand for 1 hour. The batter should be very thick.

Melt a pat of butter in a small frying pan over medium heat. Pour one-quarter of the batter into the pan and spread it flat with a spoon. Reduce the heat to medium-low. Cook for 2–3 minutes, or until the underside is golden. Flip the pancake and cook for another couple of minutes until cooked through. Transfer to a plate and keep warm while you make the rest of the pancakes.

Garnish with walnuts and serve immediately with butter and maple syrup or butternut squash preserve and its syrup. These can also be eaten cold.

WINTER

Winter begins in Iran with the festival of Yaldā, which falls on the eve of the winter solstice, and finishes with Nōrūz, which falls on March 21st, marking the first day of spring. All the festivals celebrated during winter are associated with fire and light, including the main one—Chārshanbeh Sūri—which is celebrated all over Iran.

Chārshanbeh Sūri is held on the last Tuesday of the Persian calendar year, which ends on March 20th. Just after sunset, children and young people gather in the streets and light bonfires. Everybody, even the elderly, will then go out and jump over the fire, while reciting lines of verse—"zardī-ye man az to, sorkhī-ye to az man"—asking it to take away their pallor and sickness and give them health, warmth, and energy. After the Islamic Revolution of 1979, Iran's clerical establishment tried very hard to suppress these festivities, which they associated with pre-Islamic traditions, but the more they tried, the more defiant and raucous the youth became—and the bigger the bonfires in the streets. In the past few years, they have slightly relaxed their restrictions.

After jumping over the fire, everyone goes home to celebrate late into the night with candles, poetry, music and, of course, a feast. My family always served herbed rice and pan-fried fish for Chārshanbeh Sūridinner, while my husband's family had rice with ghormeh sabzī, a very green lamb stew, served with smoked fish. The green color of these dishes symbolizes the green crops people hope for in the coming year.

Nuts, dried fruit, and a rose-flavored sweet called bāslōgh (similar to Turkish delight) are mixed to make a popular Chārshanbeh Sūri treat, which is shared with family and friends and given to revelers who go from door to door banging their spoons on metal pots and pans.

Winter food in Iran is rich and hearty with lots of legumes, dried fruits, nuts, and wheat noodles, making good use of whatever fruits and vegetables were preserved or dried in the more plentiful months. Hearty soups like āsh reshteh, sweet and sour noodle soup with fruit and nuts (āsh-e mīveh), rice dishes adorned with dried fruit, sweet dates, and nuts, and dishes enriched with kashk—a very high-protein dairy product made from yogurt—are enjoyed, as are high-calorie desserts and sweets made with dates and nuts and lots of butter and oil; all foods designed to help keep people warm and healthy through the colder, darker months of winter.

Winter recipes

Āsh-e Anār
Pomegranate Soup

This delicious soup is often made for Yaldā, on the eve of the Winter Solstice. Āsh-e anār can be made with fresh pomegranate seeds and juice or pomegranate molasses—in this recipe I've used both. The original recipe calls for tareh (Persian chives). Chives or tender leek leaves are often used instead, but I've recently discovered that kale works as an excellent substitute in this soup.

SERVES 4–6

2 onions, chopped

3 tablespoons oil

1½ teaspoons ground turmeric

4 cups (1 liter) boiling water or beef stock

¼ cup (1¾ oz/50 g) Thai jasmine or Arborio rice

⅓ cup (2 oz/60 g) Persian yellow lentils or chana dal, washed and soaked for 30 minutes

1⅔ cups (3½ oz/100 g) cilantro, coarsely chopped

⅓ cup (¾ oz/20 g) flat-leaf parsley, coarsely chopped

¾ cup (1¾ oz/50 g) coarsely chopped tareh (Persian chives) or kale

½ quantity tiny meatballs (page 282, optional)

2 tablespoons tomato paste

3 tablespoons pomegranate molasses, or to taste

Salt and black pepper

1 quantity fried mint (page 276)

¼ cup (1 oz/30 g) pomegranate seeds, to garnish

Fry the onions in the oil over medium heat until nicely golden. Add 1 teaspoon of the turmeric and continue cooking for a couple of minutes. Remove one-quarter of the onions to use as a garnish, then add the rest of the turmeric to the pot. Cook for 1 minute, then add the boiling water or stock, rice, and lentils. Bring to a boil, then lower the heat and simmer for 30 minutes. Skim off any foam. Add the cilantro, parsley, and tareh or kale and simmer for another 30 minutes.

Meanwhile, make the tiny meatballs according to the recipe on page 282, if using. When the meatballs are well browned, save a few for the garnish and add the rest to the soup, along with any oil from the pan. Add the tomato paste, pomegranate molasses, salt, and pepper. Simmer, partly covered, for 30 minutes. The rice should be very soft and the soup nice and thick.

When ready to serve, ladle the soup into a tureen or individual bowls. Garnish with the fried onions, fried mint, pomegranate seeds, and the reserved meatballs.

Āsh-e Mīveh Tabrizī

Tabrizi Noodle Soup

My grandmother on my father's side made huge pots of this luxurious soup once a year each winter, and sent bowls of it to her neighbors and any relatives who lived close by. My mother never made this soup at home so I had only a vague memory of how it tasted, but she remembered my grandmother's recipe and gave it to me a few years ago. I now make it once a year, just like she did, to keep an almost forgotten family tradition alive.

SERVES 4–6

¼ cup (60 ml) oil

3 onions, finely sliced

1½ teaspoons ground turmeric

8 cups (2 liters) boiling water or stock

10 cups (10½ oz/300 g) spinach, coarsely chopped

1 cup (2 oz/60 g) cilantro, coarsely chopped

⅔ cup (1½ oz/40 g) flat-leaf parsley, coarsely chopped

10 dried apricots

10 prunes

A handful of dried sour cherries or dried cranberries

A handful of walnuts

A handful of blanched almonds

A handful of blanched hazelnuts

1 x 15 oz (425 g) can chickpeas, drained

1 x 15 oz (425 g) can borlotti beans, drained

1 cup (3½ oz/100 g) Persian soup noodles, udon, or eggless linguini

⅔ cup (150 ml) white wine vinegar

Sugar, to taste

Fried mint, to garnish (page 276)

Heat the oil in a large deep pot or Dutch oven over medium heat and fry the onions until golden brown. Add the turmeric and swirl around for a minute. Pour in the boiling water and bring back to a boil. Add the spinach, herbs, dried fruit, nuts, chickpeas, and beans to the pot. Cover and simmer for 45 minutes or until the fruits have softened. Add the noodles and cook until they are soft and the soup has thickened— about 20 minutes. If you are using udon or linguini you may need to thicken the soup with 1 teaspoon flour dissolved in 1 tablespoon water.

Correct the seasoning and add the vinegar and as much sugar as you wish. The soup should have a delicate sweet and sour flavor. Alternatively, dissolve 3 tablespoons sugar in the vinegar over low heat and serve the vinegar syrup separately to allow everyone to flavor the soup to their liking. Pour the soup into bowls and garnish with the fried mint.

Eshkaneh-ye Keshteh
Apricot and Poached Egg Soup

You will find variations of this quick, rustic soup being made all over Iran. In the old days in winter there was very little fresh produce available, so nuts and dried fruits such as apricots, peaches, plums, raisins, and dates featured heavily in soups and stews. This soup is generally either thickened or finished with eggs, but feel free to make yours without; it will still be delicious. It's best to use lavāsh for the "croutons" in this soup, but broken matzo or even Sicilian carta di musica make excellent substitutes. Add the torn or broken bread to the soup in small amounts so it doesn't get too soggy.

SERVES 4

12 dried apricots
3½ tablespoons (1¾ oz/50 g) butter
2 onions, thinly sliced
1 teaspoon ground turmeric
3 tablespoons all-purpose flour
2 tablespoons dried mint
1 tablespoon tomato paste
6 cups (1½ liters) water
Salt and pepper, to taste
4 small eggs
Pinch of sugar, to taste (optional)
A few mint leaves, to garnish
Flatbread, to serve

Put the apricots in a bowl, cover with hot water, and leave to soak for about an hour until soft. If your apricots are already quite soft you can skip this stage.

Melt the butter over medium heat and sauté the onions until lightly browned. Add the turmeric, flour, and dried mint and cook, stirring, for a couple of minutes. Stir in the tomato paste and cook for a minute. Add the water and the drained apricots and bring to a boil. Lower the heat, then cover and simmer for 20 minutes or until the onions and apricots are very soft and the soup has thickened a little. Season well with salt and pepper.

Lower the heat as much as you can so the soup is no longer bubbling. Break one egg into a cup and gently slide it into the soup. Repeat with the rest of the eggs. Simmer without stirring until the eggs are almost set, then cover the saucepan and cook gently for 10–15 minutes until the eggs are cooked through.

Place an egg in each serving bowl and cover with the broth. Garnish with a few mint leaves and serve with some torn flatbread on top and plenty of sabzī khordan (page 98).

Eshkaneh-ye Piyāz
Egg and Onion Soup with Walnuts

This recipe is an Azarbaijani version of a very popular onion soup and was a particular favorite of my father's. At home, we'd soak torn flatbread in our soup and eat it with a dollop of yogurt, sabzī khordan (page 98), and vegetable pickles (torshī, page 262-271).

SERVES 4

3½ tablespoons (1¾ oz/50 g) butter

3 red onions, thinly sliced

1 teaspoon ground turmeric

5 cups (1.2 liters) boiling water

Salt and black pepper

Cayenne pepper

¾ cup (3 oz/80 g) walnut halves, broken into pieces

4 small eggs

Mint leaves, to garnish (optional)

Flatbread, to serve

Yogurt, to serve

Melt the butter and cook the onions over medium heat until lightly browned, stirring from time to time. Add the turmeric and stir over medium heat for 1 minute, then add the boiling water. Lower the heat, cover, and simmer for 20 minutes or until the onions are very soft and beginning to disintegrate. Taste and add salt, pepper, and cayenne pepper to your liking.

Uncover the pot and make sure the soup is not bubbling. Add the walnuts and stir through. Break the eggs one by one into a cup and slide each into the soup. Partially cover the pot and simmer very gently until the eggs are well cooked, about 10 minutes.

Place an egg in each serving bowl and cover with the hot broth. Garnish with mint and more cayenne, if desired. At the table add a handful of torn flatbread to each bowl, mix through, and top with a dollop of yogurt.

Khoresht-e Māhī Chābahārī
Chabahari Fish Stew

This quick, spicy fish stew is popular in Chabahar, a port city on the shores of the Oman Sea. The cuisine of Chabahar is influenced by the flavors of India and Pakistan, and fish features heavily in local dishes. They make this stew with kingfish (narrow-barred Spanish mackerel), a prized fish that can sometimes be more than a meter long, but any thick, meaty fish will work. My favorites are cod loins or red snapper.

SERVES 4

4 thick fish fillets with skin
½ teaspoon sea salt flakes
3 tablespoons oil
1 onion, finely chopped
2 red chili peppers
2 cloves of garlic
A big handful of cilantro
1 teaspoon ground turmeric
¼ teaspoon ground cumin
¼ teaspoon ground black pepper
¼ teaspoon cayenne pepper
¼ teaspoon ground coriander
½ teaspoon dried lime powder
2 tablespoons tomato paste
Generous ¾ cup (200 ml) boiling water
2–3 tablespoons tamarind paste
A few chopped cilantro leaves, to garnish

Sprinkle the fish with the salt and set aside. Heat the oil in a frying pan and cook the onion over medium heat for a few minutes or until it begins to color.

Put the chilies, garlic, and cilantro in a food processor and process to form a paste. Add the spices and pulse to mix. Add the paste to the onions and cook, stirring, until the spices are fragrant, about 3 minutes. Add the tomato paste and cook for 2 minutes. Add the water, cover the pan, and simmer gently for 15 minutes.

Gradually stir the tamarind paste into the sauce, tasting to make sure the sauce doesn't become too acidic. Add more salt and pepper to your liking. Arrange the fish fillets in the sauce and cover the pan. Cook very gently for 15–20 minutes, or until the fish is cooked through and flakes easily with a fork. Sprinkle with the chopped cilantro and serve with chelō (page 236) or kateh (page 239) and Baluchi mango relish (page 267).

Ghaliyeh Meygū Būshehrī
Bushehri Shrimp with Fenugreek

Prawn stews are a speciality of the southern regions of Iran. This one uses fresh fenugreek greens, which can now be found in many supermarkets or Asian grocers. You can also use this sauce for another fish stew (ghaliyeh māhī), which is usually made with grouper or mackerel fillets.

SERVES 4

3 tablespoons oil

1 onion, finely chopped

3⅓ cups (7 oz/200 g) cilantro, finely chopped

⅓ cup (¾ oz/20 g) fresh fenugreek leaves, chopped, or 1½ teaspoons dried

½ head of garlic

1 teaspoon ground turmeric

½ teaspoon cayenne pepper

1 teaspoon all-purpose flour

½ teaspoon salt

1 teaspoon black pepper

14 oz (400 g) large fresh shrimp, peeled and deveined

1–2 tablespoons tomato paste

2–3 tablespoons tamarind paste

Generous ¾ cup (200 ml) boiling water

Heat the oil in a frying pan and sauté the onions over medium heat until golden. Add the herbs and garlic and continue to cook for 5 minutes, or until the greens begin to darken and are very fragrant. Add the turmeric, cayenne, flour, salt, and pepper, and stir for a couple of minutes. Add the shrimp and continue to sauté for 4 minutes, then add the tomato paste and stir for a couple of minutes.

Dissolve the tamarind paste in the boiling water and add to the stew gradually, tasting as you go to make sure the sauce doesn't become too acidic. Bring to a boil, then lower the heat, and simmer gently for 15–20 minutes. Serve with rice or flatbread.

Khoresht-e Gheymeh
Lamb and Yellow Lentil Stew

Khoresht-e Gheymeh is a very popular stew, enjoyed throughout the year, but best suited to winter, in my view, since it contains no fresh herbs or vegetables. It is often made in large quantities for ceremonies and festivals. In a recent cooking show on Iranian television, a chef gave a recipe for Gheymeh that called for 110 kilos of lamb, 20 kilos of yellow lentils, 150 kilos of potatoes, and over a liter of rosewater. With rice, this amount would feed about a thousand people. The recipe below will only feed four.

SERVES 4

4 dried limes

2 tablespoons oil

2 onions, finely chopped

14 oz (400 g) boneless lamb neck fillet or lean shoulder, cubed

1 teaspoon ground turmeric

3 tablespoons tomato paste

⅓ stick of cinnamon

2 whole green cardamom pods, or a pinch ground cardamom

½ teaspoon salt

¼ teaspoon black pepper

2 cups (500 ml) boiling water

1¼ cups (9 oz/250 g) Persian yellow lentils (or use chana dal; see glossary entry for lapeh, page 306)

Pinch of ground saffron

½ teaspoon rosewater (optional)

Tarragon sprigs, to garnish (optional)

Place the limes in a bowl and cover them with hot water. Cover the bowl and leave to soak for a couple of hours, making sure the limes are submerged. This will remove any bitterness from their skins.

Heat the oil in a pot over medium heat and fry the onion until golden. Add the lamb and turmeric and cook until the meat is brown all over. Add the tomato paste, cinnamon, cardamom, salt, and pepper and stir for 2 minutes. Pour over the boiling water and bring back to a boil. Cover, lower the heat, and simmer for 45 minutes.

Wash the lentils, put them in a small pot, and cover with water. Bring to a boil over medium-low heat. Cook until al dente (check package instructions; cooking times vary). Drain well and rinse. Set aside.

Drain the limes and, with a sharp knife, cut a small slice from the top or make a few slits on their sides. Tuck them into the stew. Cover and simmer for 20–30 minutes or until the lamb is soft. Discard the cinnamon and cardamom pods.

Add the saffron, rosewater, and drained lentils to the stew and stir. Cover and continue to simmer over very low heat for about 15 minutes or until the lentils are completely cooked. Transfer the stew to a serving dish, garnish with tarragon (if using), and serve with chelō (page 236) or kateh (page 239), and sīb zamīnī sorkh kardeh (page 281).

Khoresht-e Gerdū Esfenāj
Lamb in Walnut, Pomegranate, and Spinach Sauce

This sophisticated dish is a speciality of Dāmghān, the ancient Hecatompylos, in central Iran. The stew is similar to the northern Iranian fesenjūn (page 197) and, like fesenjūn, it needs to cook long and slow to allow the walnuts to release their delicious oil. This improves in flavor by sitting in the fridge, and can be made up to three days in advance, making it one of my go-to dishes for entertaining.

SERVES 4-6

¼ cup (60 ml) oil

2 onions, finely chopped

1 lb (500 g) boneless lamb neck fillet or lean shoulder, cut into chunks

1 teaspoon ground turmeric

½ teaspoon mild curry powder

2 tablespoons tomato paste

1 cinnamon stick

Boiling water

3¾ cups (10½ oz/300 g) ground walnuts

½ teaspoon salt

1 lb 5 oz (600 g) spinach

1 cup (250 ml) pomegranate molasses

Slivered pistachios and micro-greens, to garnish (optional)

Heat the oil in a heavy pot or Dutch oven and lightly brown the onions. Add the meat, turmeric, and curry powder and fry until the meat is lightly browned all over. Add the tomato paste and the cinnamon stick along with enough boiling water to cover the meat by a fingertip. Add the ground walnuts and salt, then cover and simmer for 1½ hours, stirring occasionally.

Wash and finely chop the spinach, then wilt in a small pan. Drain off any excess water, then add to the lamb along with the pomegranate molasses. Simmer gently, stirring once or twice, until the lamb is very tender and the sauce has the consistency of thick gravy—this will take around 1 hour. Add a small amount of boiling water if the sauce becomes too thick. Garnish with pistachios and microgreens, if desired, and serve with chelō (page 236) or kateh (page 239).

Tās Kabāb-e Beh

Slow-Cooked Lamb, Eggplant, and Quince Hotpot

Tās kabāb is always slow-cooked to bring out the complex flavors of the lamb, quince, and spices. For a perfect tās kabāb, the lamb must cook until it shreds easily with a fork and the sauce needs to reduce to the consistency of gravy.

SERVES 4-6

4 tablespoons oil or melted butter

6 onions, peeled and thickly sliced

14 oz (400 g) boneless lamb shoulder or leg, trimmed of excess fat and thickly sliced

1½ tablespoons sumac, plus extra to serve

1 teaspoon ground turmeric

¾ teaspoon salt

½ teaspoon black pepper

2 eggplants, thickly sliced

4 cloves of garlic, sliced

1 large quince, peeled, cored, and sliced

7 oz (200 g) cherry tomatoes, halved

¼ cup (60 ml) water

1 tablespoon tomato paste

2 potatoes, peeled and sliced

Parsley sprigs, to garnish (optional)

Pour 2 tablespoons of the oil or butter into a large saucepan and arrange half of the onion slices on the bottom. Lay the meat over the onions.

In a bowl, mix the sumac, turmeric, salt, and black pepper. Sprinkle one-third of the spice mix over the meat in the pot, then top with the rest of the onions. Arrange the sliced eggplants on top. Add the garlic, then sprinkle with another third of the spice mix. Layer on the quince, then add the rest of the spice mix and the cherry tomatoes. Mix the water with the tomato paste and the rest of the oil and pour into the pot. Cover tightly and cook over low heat for 1½ hours.

Remove the lid and arrange the potato slices on top, spooning over some of the juices. Continue cooking, covered, over low heat for 30 minutes or until the potatoes are tender and most of the juices from the vegetables have evaporated. Sprinkle with a little more sumac, garnish with parsley, if using, and serve with bread and salad.

Dolmeh-ye Kalam-e Malas

Sweet and Sour Cabbage Rolls

This popular dish has many variations. In this recipe, a syrup of vinegar and sugar (serkeh shīreh) flavored with saffron gives the dolmeh their unique flavor. The best cabbages for stuffing are the very large flat white ones you find in Middle Eastern grocery stores. If all you can find are round cabbages, buy the largest one possible. Any extra leaves can be put to good use later in soups.

SERVES 4–6

1 large white cabbage, cored
Boiling water
½ cup (3½ oz/100 g) Thai jasmine rice
3 tablespoons oil
2 onions, chopped
9 oz (250 g) lean ground beef
¾ teaspoon salt
½ teaspoon cinnamon
1 teaspoon ground cumin
1 teaspoon ground turmeric
½ teaspoon black pepper
¼ teaspoon cayenne pepper
1 cup (3½ oz/100 g) currants or small raisins
⅓ cup (1¾ oz/50 g) barberries
12 dried apricots (optional)
½ cup (120 ml) white wine vinegar
2–3 tablespoons sugar, or to taste
Large pinch of saffron
1 tablespoon (½ oz/15 g) butter

Put the cabbage in a pot and cover with boiling water. Cook for 15 minutes, then drain and rinse with cold water. Gently pull each leaf from the base; you will need 10–15 large leaves.

Rinse the rice to remove any excess starch. Bring 1¾ cups (400 ml) water to a boil in a saucepan with a ¼ teaspoon of salt and cook the rice until it's just softening, about 5 minutes. Drain and set aside. Heat the oil in a frying pan and sauté the onions until golden. Add the meat, ½ teaspoon of salt, and all the spices and cook until the meat is lightly browned. Stir in the raisins, two-thirds of the barberries, and all of the rice and mix.

Cover the bottom of a deep frying pan with two layers of small or broken cabbage leaves. To stuff the leaves, place one on a board with the rib end facing you. Place 3–4 tablespoons of the filling onto the leaf, then fold the bottom of the leaf over. Bring in the two sides and roll it up like a spring roll. Arrange the stuffed leaves in the pan, tucking the apricots between them, and cover with another layer of broken cabbage leaves. Add enough water to almost cover, then place a small plate on top to keep everything in place. Cover and bring to a boil over low heat, then reduce the heat to very low and braise for 1½ hours until almost all of the water has been absorbed.

In a small saucepan, bring the vinegar and sugar to a boil. Add the saffron and salt and stir to dissolve. Pour it over the cabbage rolls, then cover and continue to braise for another 20 minutes, basting occasionally, until the sauce has reduced by half. Melt the butter in a small saucepan and toss the remaining barberries in it. Cook for a minute to puff them up. Garnish with the barberries and serve warm or cold.

Anār Dāneh Mossammā
Chicken with Pomegranate

My fascination with the food from Gilan, a narrow, fertile strip of land enclosed between the Caspian Sea and the Alborz mountains, started with this chicken stew. The sauce, flavored with sour plums and the tart pomegranate seeds so abundant during winter, is fruity, pleasantly sour, and truly delicious.

SERVES 4

4 whole chicken legs, or 8 small thighs

¾ teaspoon salt

2 tablespoons (1 oz/30 g) butter

3 tablespoons oil

2 small red onions, finely chopped

Seeds from 1 large pomegranate

1 teaspoon ground turmeric

2 tablespoons tomato paste

6 red plums, pitted and chopped

A few slivered pistachios or chopped parsley, to garnish

Sprinkle the chicken with the salt. Melt the butter in a heavy-bottomed pot or deep frying pan and brown the chicken until golden on both sides. Remove from the pan and set aside.

Add the oil to the pan and gently fry the onions until golden brown. Save 2 tablespoons of the pomegranate seeds for the garnish and add the rest to the onions along with the turmeric. Continue to cook for a few minutes, then add the tomato paste and cook for 2 minutes. Return the chicken and any juices to the pan. Add enough water to almost cover the meat. Simmer gently while you make the plum purée.

Put the chopped plums in a small saucepan with ½ cup (120 ml) water. Cover and cook over medium heat until the water is evaporated and the plums are very soft. Pass through a sieve or process in a food processor to purée.

Add the plum purée to the chicken and stir through. Simmer for 30 minutes or until the sauce is thick and the chicken is falling from the bone. Add a little boiling water during cooking if the sauce gets too thick and add a little salt, if required. Garnish with the reserved pomegranate seeds and slivered pistachios or chopped parsley. Serve with chelō (page 236) or kateh (page 239), some sliced white radishes, and olives.

Fesenjūn-e Ordak
Duck with Walnut, Squash, and Pomegranate

Fesenjūn is considered by many to be the queen of Iranian dishes. It's usually made in colder months because walnuts are a "hot" food (see page xv). The dish has many variations and is often made with game birds, chicken, or even tiny meatballs (page 282). I find bone-in duck or chicken legs work best—the meat should be cooked until it almost falls off the bone. In Gilan, where the dish probably originated, they like the sauce very dark, so they sometimes drop a heated horseshoe or large iron nail into the pot to interact with the tannins from the walnuts and pomegranate and darken the color of the dish. Try this at home if you're feeling adventurous.

SERVES 4

4 duck legs

Salt and black pepper

2 tablespoons oil

4 cups (14 oz/400 g) walnuts

Ice cubes (as required)

10½ oz (300 g) butternut squash, peeled and cut into small cubes

3 tablespoons tomato paste

1 cup (250 ml) pomegranate molasses

Sugar, to taste

Pomegranate seeds, to garnish (optional)

Rub the duck legs with salt and a little pepper. Heat the oil in a large heavy-bottomed pan over medium-high heat until hot. Put the duck legs in the pan one by one, allowing the pan to get hot before adding the next one. Fry until golden all over. Remove from the pan and set aside.

Put the walnuts in a food processor and pulse several times until well ground. Toast in the pan over medium heat until warm and fragrant, stirring constantly to avoid burning them. Remove the skin from the duck legs if you wish and return the legs to the pan with any juices. Add enough water to just cover, bring to a boil, then turn the heat down to very low and simmer for 1½ hours, stirring from time to time. Halfway through cooking, drop a few ice cubes into the sauce to help release the oil from the walnuts.

Add the squash to the stew. Simmer for another 1 hour, stirring from time to time.

Once the squash is soft, use a spoon to mash it into the sauce. Add the tomato paste and enough of the pomegranate molasses to make the sauce milk-chocolate brown. Simmer until the duck legs are tender and the sauce has thickened and darkened. Taste and add more pomegranate molasses if needed and a little sugar if the sauce is too sour. Garnish with a few pomegranate seeds and serve with chelō (page 236) or kateh (page 239), sabzī khordan (page 98), and pickled vegetables (shūr, page 273).

Gondī
Persian Jewish Chicken Dumplings

Gondī is very popular among the Jewish community still living in Iran, as well as those who left after the Islamic revolution, which led to the migration of around 60,000 Jews. This simple dish is given an exotic twist through the addition of spices—cardamom, cinnamon, and cumin. The broth is eaten separately with torn flatbread, then the gondī are rolled in flatbread with sabzī khordan (page 98) and torshī (page 262-271).

SERVES 4

6 cups (1½ liters) chicken stock

1 teaspoon ground turmeric

2 dried limes, pierced in several places

1 stalk celery

A few sprigs of parsley

1 red chili pepper (optional)

1 lb (500 g) boneless chicken thighs and breasts, cubed

3 tablespoons chickpea flour or besan

¼ teaspoon ground cardamom

½ teaspoon cinnamon

¼ teaspoon ground cumin

1 teaspoon dried mint, crushed

1 teaspoon dried tarragon, crushed

1 onion, grated

½ teaspoon salt, plus more to taste

¼ teaspoon ground black pepper, plus more to taste

Bring the stock to a boil with half of the turmeric and the dried limes, celery, parsley, and chili, if using. Lower the heat and allow to simmer gently while you prepare the dumplings.

In a food processor, combine the chicken, chickpea flour, the rest of the turmeric, the spices, herbs, grated onion, salt, and pepper, in a food processor and process until the chicken is finely chopped and the ingredients are well mixed. Divide the mixture into four equal portions. Dip your hands in cold water and shape each portion into a round dumpling. Drop the dumplings into the simmering stock.

Cover and simmer over very low heat for at least 1½ hours, until very tender. The dumplings don't need to be completely submerged but do turn them once or twice. The longer and slower they cook, the better they will taste.

Once done, taste the broth and add more salt and pepper if needed. Discard the celery, parsley, and chili pepper, and serve.

Kalam Polō

Rice with Beef and Cabbage

Though some dislike the smell of cooked cabbage, this comforting spiced rice dish smells so good that even the most serious cabbage haters will be drawn to the kitchen. In Iran, if a neighbor is pregnant, it is customary to send them a plateful of any strongly smelling food you might be cooking, since we believe that cravings must always be satisfied to avoid harming the baby. This is exactly the sort of dish that can cause—and relieve—serious cravings.

SERVES 4

2 cups (14 oz/400 g) white long grain rice

14 oz (400 g) white cabbage, coarsely chopped

5 tablespoons oil

2 small onions, finely chopped

7 oz (200 g) lean ground beef

1 teaspoon ground turmeric

½ teaspoon ground black pepper

½ teaspoon ground cumin

⅓ cup (80 ml) tomato paste

½ teaspoon smoked sea salt

Generous ¾ cup (200 ml) boiling water

Torn flatbread or thick slices of potato (optional)

1½ tablespoons (¾ oz/20 g) butter

Cook the rice according to the instructions for making chelō (page 236). Leave to drain in a colander. Sauté the cabbage in 1 tablespoon of the oil over medium heat for 5 minutes, until it begins to brown at the edges. Remove from the pan and set aside. Add 2 more tablespoons of the oil and fry the onions. Once lightly colored, add the meat, turmeric, pepper, and cumin and cook until well browned. Add the tomato paste, smoked salt, fried cabbage, and the boiling water. Cover and simmer gently until all the water is absorbed.

Put the remaining 2 tablespoons oil in a nonstick pot over high heat. Arrange a layer of flatbread or potatoes in the hot oil. Remove from the heat. Gently transfer one-third of the rice to the pot in a mound. Arrange one-third of the cabbage mixture on top. Repeat with the rest of the ingredients. Wrap the lid in a clean dish towel and cover the pot. Heat over medium-high heat until the side of the pot is hot and sizzles when touched with a wet finger, then turn the heat down very low and watch for signs of steam.

Melt the butter with 2 tablespoons water and pour it over the rice. Cover again and let the rice steam without lifting the lid. Gently tap the top of the mound approximately 30 minutes after the first signs of steam appear from the top of the rice. It will "tremble" a little if it's ready. Alternatively, once the butter is added, the covered pot can also cook on the lowest rack of an oven preheated to 325°F (170°C) for 30 minutes.

Transfer the rice to a platter and arrange the crispy flatbread or potato tahdīg around the sides. Serve with some yogurt, mixed torshī (page 262–271), and lots of sabzī khordan (page 98).

Morassa' Polō
Jeweled Rice

Jeweled rice looks beautiful and is surprisingly easy to make. Elaborate versions of this dish were served on banquet days in the courts of the Safavid kings in the fifteenth century. Court chefs decorated morassa' polō with intricate patterns made with dates, figs, green raisins, nuts, chickpeas, and lentils, and hid pieces of succulent lamb or chicken between the layers of rice. The garnishes became so exaggerated that one court chef openly criticized his fellow chefs for overstating the importance of garnishing at the cost of actual cooking skills.

SERVES 4–6

2 cups (14 oz/400 g) white long grain rice

½ cup (1¾ oz/50 g) slivered almonds

2 tablespoons rosewater

2 large oranges, or 3 Seville oranges

scant ½ cup (3 oz/80 g) sugar, for cooking the peel

½ cup (120 ml) water

1½ tablespoons (¾ oz/20 g) butter

⅓ cup (1¾ oz/50 g) barberries

1–2 tablespoons sugar for the barberries (optional)

½ teaspoon saffron water (page 278)

½ cup (1¾ oz/50 g) slivered pistachios

Cook the rice according to the instructions for chelō (page 236). While the rice is steaming, soak the almond slivers in rosewater diluted with 2 tablespoons hot water.

Use a vegetable peeler or sharp knife to remove long strips of peel from the oranges. Cut off any white pith, then slice the peel very thinly. Place a saucepan on the heat and fill with boiling water. Drop the peel into the water and cook for 2 minutes. Drain in a colander. Repeat two or three times until the peel no longer tastes bitter. Refresh in cold water and drain well. Put the sugar and water in the saucepan and bring to a boil. Add the peel and cook for 5 minutes or until the syrup is thick and bubbly. Turn off the heat and set aside.

When you are ready to serve, drain the almond slivers and set aside. Melt half of the butter in a small saucepan over medium heat and add the almonds. Heat through without coloring, then remove from the pan and set aside. Melt the rest of the butter and add the barberries with 1 or 2 tablespoons sugar (if using). Swirl around for a couple of minutes to puff up the berries and dissolve the sugar.

Drain the orange peel. Put a few spoonfuls of cooked rice in a small bowl and mix with the saffron water, then add the barberries, peel, almonds, and pistachios. Layer the saffron rice mixture with the plain rice on a platter. Alternatively, mound the plain rice on a platter and use the saffron rice, fruit, and nuts to create a pattern on top. Lift the crispy rice from the bottom of the pot and serve separately.

Reshteh Polō
Rice with Toasted Noodles

This is traditionally prepared for Persian new year because of the dish's symbolic meaning. The word for noodles (reshteh) also means "string," so the noodles here represent holding onto, or untangling, the strings of life so you won't get confused or lost in the year ahead. The dish would also be served when a suitor visited the family of his bride-to-be in order to "talk business" in preparation for a long and happy marriage. The garnish is optional, but makes the dish look really special.

SERVES 4–6

2 cups (14 oz/400 g) white long grain rice

1½ cups (5 oz/150 g) Persian noodles for rice (reshte-ye polōī), vermicelli, or capellini

2 tablespoons oil

3 tablespoons (1½ oz/40 g) butter

½ teaspoon saffron water (page 278)

FOR THE GARNISH

1½ tablespoons (¾ oz/20 g) butter

½ cup (1¾ oz/50 g) currants or small raisins, soaked in cold water

12 dates, pitted

12 small dried apricots

Wash and soak the rice according to the instructions for chelō (page 236). If using vermicelli or capellini, break them into 4 inch (10 cm) pieces, spread on a baking tray, and toast in the oven for a few minutes until golden, stirring a couple of times so they color evenly (Persian noodles for rice are ready-toasted). Boil the rice according to the instructions for chelō. If you're using vermicelli or capellini, add them to the pot as soon as the water comes to the boil; Persian noodles for rice should be added once the rice grains begin to float to the surface. Drain the rice as soon as the noodles soften—they should still have a little bite to them. Rinse with lukewarm water to stop them cooking further.

Heat the oil over medium heat in a large saucepan until very hot. Transfer the rice to the pot, mounding it in the middle. Wrap the lid in a dish towel and cover the pan. Increase the heat and cook for a couple of minutes or until the side of the pot sizzles when touched with a wet finger. Reduce the heat to low.

Melt the butter with 2 tablespoons water and pour it over the rice. Cover the pot right away. Lower the heat as much as you can and let the rice steam. Gently tap the top of the mound of rice approximately 30 minutes after the first signs of steam appear. It will "tremble" a little if it's perfectly done.

Meanwhile prepare the garnish. Melt the butter in a small pan and cook the currants, dates, and apricots for a minute until shiny. Transfer the rice to a serving dish. Put a few tablespoons of rice in a small bowl and stir in the saffron water. Spoon this over the rest of the rice and top with the garnish. Remove the crispy rice tahdīg from the pot and serve alongside. Serve with your preferred khoresht (stew) or braised meat dish.

Damī-ye Adas

Rice and Green Lentils with Brown Butter Eggs

I like to serve this like a Persian Buddha bowl, with the rice, tahdīg, dates, and currants topped with a delicious brown butter egg. Make sure to lay out plenty of small dishes and condiments on the side, such as chopped tomato and cucumber salad (page 250), vinegary pickles (page 262-271), and sabzī khordan (page 98).

SERVES 4

2 cups (14 oz/400 g) white long grain rice

3½ cups (830 ml) water

2 teaspoons smoked sea salt

¼ cup (60 ml) oil

1 cup (7 oz/200 g) French green lentils

12 dates

6½ tablespoons (3¼ oz/90 g) butter

1¼ cups (5 oz/150 g) small currants

4 eggs

Salt and black pepper

Red pepper flakes (optional)

Put the rice in a lidded saucepan. Fill with cold water, swirl, then pour off the cloudy water and fill again. Gently rub the rice between your palms a few times. Drain the rice in a sieve and return to the pot. Add the measured water, salt, and oil, and leave to soak for at least 30 minutes. Rinse the lentils and cook in salted water until almost soft, about 15 minutes. Drain well. Bring the rice to a boil over medium heat. Add the lentils, stir gently, and return to a boil. Cook uncovered until all the water is absorbed, 15–20 minutes.

Arrange the dates on top of the rice. Wrap the lid in a dish towel and cover the saucepan. Lower the heat and let the rice steam over medium-low heat. The rice is ready when the rice on the side of the pot is a little crispy and beginning to color. The cooking time will depend on how big or small your stove burner is but 30–40 minutes will usually be enough.

Melt 1 tablespoon (½ oz/15 g) of the butter in a small saucepan and lightly sauté the currants until shiny. Transfer to a small bowl. Remove the dates from the steamed rice and transfer to a small dish. Put a flat plate on top of the rice pot and, holding tight with both hands, invert the saucepan and the plate to release the rice cake onto the plate.

Melt the remaining butter in a heavy-bottomed large frying pan. Cook over medium heat until the butter is beginning to brown, then break in the eggs and cook until their edges are crispy and golden. Season with salt, pepper, and red pepper flakes, if desired. Garnish the rice cake with the dates and currants and serve with the fried eggs and other accompaniments.

Jūshpara Bojnordī
Dumpling Soup

I was born in Tehran, but when I was still a baby my father's job in the royal army took us to Bojnourd, a small town in the northeast. While living there, my mother fell in love with a local dumpling soup. As an adult, I visited Bojnourd several times, but could never find the soup. I finally got this recipe from a friend's mother, and my mom tells me it is just as she remembered. These jūshpara (dumplings) are flavored with fennel seeds and cumin, but there are many variations found all over the northeast. The dumplings freeze well between layers of waxed paper. Allow them to come to room temperature before boiling.

SERVES 4

FOR THE DOUGH

1⅔ cups (7 oz/200 g) 00 pasta flour (substitute all-purpose if you can't find it)

¼ teaspoon salt

½ cup (120 ml) water at room temperature

FOR THE FILLING AND SAUCE

5 cups (5 oz/150 g) spinach, coarsely chopped

4 tablespoons oil

1 onion, finely chopped

¼ teaspoon ground turmeric

½ teaspoon ground cumin

½ teaspoon fennel seeds

½ teaspoon ground coriander seeds

Scant ½ cup (1 oz/30 g) ground walnuts

1½ teaspoons salt

6 tablespoons cooked green French lentils (from about 4 tablespoons raw)

Yogurt, chopped walnuts, and red pepper flakes, to serve (optional)

To make the dough, sift the flour and salt into a bowl. Make a well in the center and gradually add the water until a sticky dough forms. Knead the dough until it doesn't stick to your hands anymore (you may need to add a tablespoon more flour). Turn the dough out onto a board lightly dusted with flour and knead for 10 minutes until silky and elastic. Shape into a ball, cover, and allow to rest for at least 30 minutes.

To make the filling and sauce, wilt the spinach in a large frying pan with 1 tablespoon water. Drain in a sieve, pressing with the back of a spoon to extract as much water as you can. Heat 1 tablespoon of the oil in the pan and brown the onion. Add all the spices and stir. Cook for a minute, then remove from the heat. Add the spinach, ground walnuts, and ½ teaspoon of the salt and mix well to form a paste. Reserve one-quarter of the mixture for the sauce and add the rest to the lentils for the filling.

To make the dumplings, divide the dough into four. Roll out one piece at a time on a surface lightly dusted with flour until it's about 1 mm thick. Cut the sheet into rectangles 2 inches (5 cm) wide and 8 inches (20 cm) long. With the long side of the rectangle facing you, place small balls of the filling (about the size of a hazelnut) near the bottom of the sheet, about ½ inch (1½ cm) apart. Carefully fold the top over the filling to cover, then fold over the bottom edge to seal the filling securely. Press your finger between each mound, then cut with

a knife to separate the dumplings. Use a small fork to press the two ends shut. Set the dumplings on a dish towel as you go. Repeat with the rest of the dough and filling.

Fill a medium saucepan with water, add the remaining 1 teaspoon salt, and bring to a boil. Add the dumplings and stir gently. Cook for 5 minutes or until they rise to the top. Drain in a colander over a bowl to catch the cooking broth.

For the sauce, heat the remaining oil over medium heat in the saucepan. Add the reserved spinach mixture and cook, stirring, for about 4 minutes. Add a few ladles of the dumpling cooking liquid to loosen the spinach mixture. You can make this thick like a sauce or thin it with water or stock to make a soup. Taste and add salt and pepper to your liking. Add the dumplings and stir well to coat. Cook for 1–2 minutes to heat through and serve with a dollop of yogurt and a sprinkling of chopped walnuts and red pepper flakes, if you wish.

Kashk-e Bādemjūn
Eggplant and Kashk with Crispy Garlic and Walnuts

This delicious dip is one of the oldest Persian dishes and quite an adventure for the tastebuds for non-Middle Easterners. You will either love it or hate it. The flavor of kashk is very hard to describe; it's salty and a bit tangy. The closest comparison that comes to my mind is the flavor of Norwegian brunost. If you can't find kashk, or don't like the taste, use yogurt instead. Just cook the eggplants with the rest of the ingredients and dress with plain yogurt after mashing.

SERVES 4-6

4 eggplants

4–6 tablespoons oil

2 onions, chopped

½ teaspoon ground turmeric

Scant ½ cup (100 ml) boiling water

4 cloves of garlic, finely chopped

½ teaspoon black pepper

3½ tablespoons (50 ml) kashk, plus more if you wish

Salt, if needed

½ cup (1¾ oz/50 g) chopped walnuts

½ quantity fried mint (page 276)

½ quantity fried garlic (page 276)

A few drops of saffron water (page 278, optional)

Preheat the oven to 350°F (180°C). Peel the eggplants and cut them in half lengthways. Brush generously with 2–3 tablespoons of the oil and roast for 20–30 minutes until golden brown and soft.

Fry the onions in the remaining 3 tablespoons of the oil over medium heat until golden. Add the turmeric and fry for another 2 minutes. Reserve one-third of the onions for garnishing then add the eggplants to the fried onions in the pan, along with the water, garlic, and pepper. Simmer over low heat for 30 minutes, covered. Add a little more boiling water from the kettle if it starts to catch on the bottom. Use a potato masher or fork to break up the eggplants. Cook for a few more minutes until the mixture is quite thick.

Add the kashk and stir. Taste and add salt if needed. Transfer the dip to a serving dish and garnish with more kashk, the reserved fried onions, chopped walnuts, fried mint, fried garlic, and a few drops of saffron water. Serve hot or cold with warm flatbread.

Bādemjān bā Anār
Eggplant, Pomegranate, and Walnut Stew

Eggplants are sometimes called "the black chicken" in Gilan. Like its meaty relatives, this stew is delicately spiced with turmeric, cinnamon, and saffron—just the kind of smell you want to fill your house with on a cold winter day. My method for frying eggplants below is meant to minimize the amount of oil used for frying, since they tend to soak up a lot of it.

SERVES 4

3 medium eggplants

6 tablespoons oil

2 onions, finely chopped

1 teaspoon ground turmeric

¼ teaspoon ground black pepper

1 tablespoon tomato paste

½ cup (1¾ oz/50 g) chopped walnuts

Seeds of 1 pomegranate

½ teaspoon salt, plus more if needed

1 cup (250 ml) boiling water

3 tablespoons pomegranate molasses

Pinch of saffron (optional)

Sugar, to taste

Fresh herbs, to garnish

Peel the eggplants in long alternative strips and thickly slice them. Heat 2 tablespoons of the oil in a large lidded frying pan over medium heat. Arrange the eggplant slices in the pan and add 2 tablespoons water. Cover and cook for 5 minutes or until the undersides are golden brown. Uncover the pan and turn the eggplants. Add 2 tablespoons of the oil and fry until golden brown. If your pan is nonstick you shouldn't need more oil, but you can add a splash of oil if the pan gets too dry. Remove from the pan and set aside. Alternatively, brush the slices generously with oil and roast in an oven preheated to 350°F (180°C) for 20 minutes until golden brown.

Add the remaining 2 tablespoons oil to the pan and fry the onions over medium heat until golden brown. Add the turmeric, pepper, tomato paste, chopped walnuts, pomegranate seeds (reserving some for the garnish), and salt. Cook for 2 minutes. Pour in the boiling water and pomegranate molasses and add the saffron, if using, and the eggplant. Reduce the heat to very low. Cover the pan with a lid and braise for 1 hour. Taste and add sugar and salt if needed to balance the flavors. Uncover and allow the sauce to cook down and thicken to your liking. Garnish with the reserved pomegranate seeds and the herbs, and serve with chelō (page 236) or kateh (page 239).

Kūkū Sībzamīnī Tabrīzī
Saffron Potato Frittata

My grandmother's potato kūkū is one of my favorite brunch dishes. Her recipe, passed down to me from my mother, is rather unusual, since it has a layer of toasted rose petals, cinnamon, and chopped walnuts hidden inside. My grandmother always cooked her kūkūs on top of the stove, since ovens were quite rare in her time, but I'm sure she would have approved of the oven method given below—it's much easier and doesn't require her amazing flipping skills. I often make this in muffin pans to serve in individual portions. It's good both hot and cold and makes a delicious wrap with sabzī khordan (page 98) and līteh bādemjūn (page 268).

SERVES 4–6

1 lb 5 oz (600 g) baking potatoes

Salt

2 tablespoons dried rose petals

½ cup (1¾ oz/50 g) chopped walnuts

1½ teaspoons cinnamon

3 large eggs

½ teaspoon baking powder

1 tablespoon saffron water (page 278)

3 tablespoons oil

4 walnut halves, to decorate

Boil the potatoes, unpeeled, in heavily salted water. Allow to cool, then peel and mash. Put the rose petals in a dry pan and lightly toast over low heat until fragrant and brittle. Be careful not to burn them. Remove from the pan and allow to cool, then crush between your palms. Mix with the walnuts and cinnamon and set aside.

Preheat the oven to 375°F (190°C). In an electric mixer, lightly beat the eggs with ½ teaspoon salt and the baking powder (you can also do this by hand, but it will result in a denser kūkū). Stir in the mashed potatoes and saffron water and beat on medium speed for about 2 minutes.

Put 2 tablespoons of the oil in a 8 inch (20 cm) nonstick pan, cake pan, or pie dish. Place in the oven for 3–4 minutes or until a little batter dropped into the oil begins to sizzle right away. Spread half of the potato mixture in the pan. Top with the spices and cover with the rest of the mixture. Decorate with the walnut halves. Bake for 15 minutes. Remove from the oven and brush the top with the remaining 1 tablespoon oil. Return to the oven and bake for 10–15 minutes or until the top is golden. Cut into wedges to serve.

Sholeh Zard

Saffron Rice Pudding

There is a tradition in Iran that if you vow to make a certain quantity of this pudding each year, the wish you most hope for will be granted. After losing two babies to illness, my grandmother vowed to cook sholeh zard with twenty kilos of rice each year if her youngest—my father—continued to live. He did, and so, each year, huge cauldrons would appear in the courtyard of her house, and relatives would bustle around, stirring the pudding and delivering it to friends, neighbors, and those in need. After the pudding has cooled, skilled cooks traditionally use cinnamon to create inscriptions of saints' names or intricate patterns on the surface. Sholeh zard can be eaten at room temperature or cold and keeps well in the fridge for a few days.

SERVES 6-8

Generous ¾ cup (5 oz/150 g) Thai jasmine, short grain, or Arborio rice

3 whole cardamom pods

1½ tablespoons (¾ oz/20 g) butter

Small pinch of salt

Kettle of boiling water

1⅓ cups (9½ oz/270 g) sugar

1½ tablespoons rosewater, or more

2 teaspoons saffron water (page 278)

3 tablespoons slivered almonds (optional)

1½ tablespoons slivered pistachios (optional)

Cinnamon, to decorate

Put the rice in a bowl and cover with cold water. Stir, then pour off the cloudy water. Fill the bowl again and gently rub the rice between your palms. Drain and add 1½ cups (350 ml) cold water. Leave to soak for a few hours or overnight.

Crack the cardamom pods and tie them up in a piece of cheesecloth. In a saucepan, combine the rice and its soaking water with the butter, salt, and another 3¾ cups (900 ml) water. Drop the cheesecloth pouch into the pot. Stir, then cook over medium-low heat on the smallest burner of your stovetop for 1 hour, or until nearly all the water is absorbed and the rice is soft. Stir from time to time to make sure the rice doesn't catch on the bottom. If the rice hasn't softened after 1 hour, add a little more boiling water from the kettle and continue cooking. The pudding should be very thick at this stage.

Remove the cheesecloth pouch, add the sugar, and stir thoroughly. Cook over low heat for 10 minutes, stirring a few times. Add the rosewater and saffron water to the pudding and stir well. Add more saffron if the color looks too pale—the pudding should be a deep yellow. Stir in half of the almond slivers and cook for a further 10 minutes. Remove from the heat and allow the pudding to cool for 10 minutes. Ladle into individual bowls. Decorate with pistachio and almond slivers and some cinnamon just before serving.

Gātā

Sweet Armenian Walnut Loaf

When I lived in Iran I always bought gātā from an Armenian patisserie in one of Tehran's oldest neighborhoods, a few steps from Saint Sarkis Cathedral. The shop is so famous that people form long lines in the street, waiting to buy gātās, Danish pastries, and other delicious sweets. Gātā is made by Armenian Iranians at Christmas and is either filled with a layer of sweet buttery paste or a mixture of ground walnuts, sugar, and spices as in the following recipe. It is lovely eaten as is with a cup of strong tea, but for an indulgent breakfast I eat it with thick clotted cream and a thick fruit jam.

MAKES 2 LOAVES

FOR THE DOUGH

3¼ cups (14 oz/400 g) all-purpose flour

½ teaspoon salt

2 teaspoons instant yeast

9 tablespoons (4½ oz/125 g) butter, at room temperature, diced, plus more for greasing

1 cup (250 ml) thick Greek yogurt, at room temperature

1 teaspoon sugar

1 large egg

1 egg white

FOR THE FILLING

¾ cup (3½ oz/100 g) all-purpose flour

7 tablespoons (3½ oz/100 g) butter

½ cup (3½ oz/100 g) sugar

⅔ cup (2 oz/60 g) ground walnuts

½ teaspoon ground cardamom

2 teaspoons cinnamon

FOR THE GLAZE

1 large egg yolk

½ teaspoon saffron water (page 278)

To make the dough, sift the flour and salt into a bowl and stir in the yeast. In a separate bowl, beat the butter then add the yogurt, sugar, whole egg, and egg white. Gradually mix the flour into the yogurt mixture to form a soft, sticky dough. Mix with your hands until the dough stops sticking to them (you may need to add a tablespoon more flour). Turn out onto a floured board and knead for 5 minutes. Shape into a ball and put in a lightly greased bowl. Cover and allow to rest for 20 minutes, then refrigerate for 3 hours or longer. The dough can be left in the fridge overnight.

To make the filling, put the flour in a dry pan and cook over medium heat for a few minutes until lightly golden. Transfer to a bowl and mix in the rest of the filling ingredients to form a thick paste.

Preheat the oven to 350°F (180°C) and grease or line a large baking tray. Divide the dough into four pieces. Shape one piece into a ball and roll into a 6 inch (15 cm) circle. Top with half of the filling, spreading it out with the back of a spoon, leaving a rim around the edge. Brush the rim with a little water and cover with another piece of dough rolled to the same size. Use a fork to press the pieces together and cut around the circle with a knife to tidy the edge. Place on the baking tray. Repeat to make the other loaf with the other two pieces of dough and the remaining filling. Cut patterns into the top of each loaf. Mix the egg yolk with saffron water and brush over the pastries.

Bake on the middle rack of the oven for 20–30 minutes or until golden brown. Allow to cool before serving.

Ranginak

Date, Walnut, and Cinnamon Dessert

This lovely dessert is quick to whip up and delicious with a cup of tea after a meal. Ranginak hails from the southern provinces of Iran where sweet dates grow in abundance. Iranian Mazāfatī dates, available from most Middle Eastern grocers and online, are perfect for making ranginak as they are sweet and very soft. If you can't find them, soak your dates in hot water to soften and dry well before assembling the dessert.

SERVES 6-8

15 walnut halves

30 dates, pitted

Small pinch of salt

1¼ cups (5 oz/150 g) all-purpose flour

½ teaspoon ground cardamom

½ teaspoon cinnamon, plus extra for sprinkling

9 tablespoons (4½ oz/125 g) butter, melted

Slivered pistachios, to decorate (optional)

Confectioner's sugar, to decorate

Break the walnut halves into two pieces and stuff each date with a piece of walnut.

In a frying pan, combine the salt and flour and toast over medium heat, stirring occasionally, until the flour becomes fragrant and is blond in color. Stir in the spices. Pour the melted butter over the flour and stir to combine. Continue to cook, stirring, until the roux is a dark brown color. Remove from the heat and allow to cool for a few minutes.

Put a few tablespoons of the spiced roux on a small plate and spread evenly, leaving the edge of the plate clear. Arrange the dates on their sides over the top, starting from the center and working towards the edge. If your dates aren't very sweet, sprinkle them with 1 or 2 tablespoons of confectioner's sugar. Pour the rest of the spiced roux evenly over the dates. Sprinkle over some cinnamon and allow to cool completely. Decorate with slivered pistachio nuts and confectioner's sugar, then cut into wedges to serve.

Khāgineh-ye Gol
Rose Petal Pancakes

Rose petal pancakes drenched in grape molasses (shīre-ye angūr) are a specialty of my mother's hometown Tabriz, where they are eaten as a dessert or for breakfast. Grape molasses is a sticky dark brown sweetener known since Roman times and still widely used in Middle Eastern, Turkish, Greek, and Persian cuisines. It's available from health food stores and online. Honey or golden syrup are good substitutes.

SERVES 4

½ loosely packed cup (⅓ oz/ 10 g) dried rose petals, plus extra to serve

3 tablespoons all-purpose flour

2 tablespoons ground walnuts

½ teaspoon baking powder

⅛ teaspoon baking soda

Pinch of salt

2 medium eggs

3 tablespoons plain yogurt

1½ tablespoons (¾ oz/20 g) butter, melted

Grape molasses, honey, or golden syrup

Put the rose petals in a small frying pan and place over low heat. Cook for a few minutes, stirring all the time, until the petals are fragrant and brittle. Be careful not to burn them. Remove from the pan and allow to cool. Rub them to a powder between your palms. In a small bowl, mix the powdered rose petals, flour, ground walnuts, baking powder, baking soda, and salt. Whisk the eggs and yogurt lightly and add them to the dry ingredients.

Place a deep frying pan over medium heat and add half of the butter. Pour the batter into the pan and allow it to cook until set and the bottom is golden. Flip the pancake over and drizzle the rest of the butter around the edge of the pan. Remove the pan from the heat when the underside is golden. Prick the pancake with a fork a few times and drizzle generously with grape molasses, honey, or golden syrup while it is still hot. Garnish with a few rose petals and serve immediately.

Halvā-ye Gol

Rose Petal and Almond Halva

Roses have long been prized in Iran—in classical poetry the rose is a metaphor for pure and perfect beauty, and the flower had pride of place in the legendary walled gardens of the ancient Persians. Roses are essential not only to our cultural identity, but also to our pantries. This sweet, fudge-like paste hails from Azarbaijan. It is traditionally eaten with a small spoon but can also be molded into shapes or piped into chocolate cases. I like to shape halvā-ye gol into little disks with a small dimple on top to hold a garnish of rose petals and chopped pistachio, and serve them with dark strong tea.

MAKES 36

1 cup (¾ oz/25 g) dried rose petals

5 tablespoons (2½ oz/70 g) butter

¼ cup (60 ml) vegetable oil

1¼ cups (5 oz/150 g) all-purpose flour

½ cup (1¾ oz/50 g) ground almonds

Small pinch of salt

¾ cup (3½ oz/100 g) confectioner's sugar

¼ cup (60 ml) rosewater

1 tablespoon finely chopped pistachios, to garnish

Save 2 tablespoons of the rose petals for garnishing the halvā. Crush the rest by rubbing them between your palms. If the petals are not completely dry, heat a frying pan and spread the rose petals in it. Turn off the heat and stir the petals until they are dry and brittle before crushing them.

In a large heavy-bottomed frying pan melt the butter with the oil over medium heat. Add the flour, ground almonds, and salt and cook, stirring constantly, for 10 minutes or until the flour is fragrant and turning blond. Allow to cool for 5 minutes then add the confectioner's sugar and the crushed rose petals and stir well. Gradually add the rosewater to form a paste—you can do this in a food processor if you like. The paste must be as pliable as soft bread dough.

Roll the mixture into small balls and gently press each ball into the shape of a thick disk with an indentation in the top. Garnish with rose petals and chopped pistachios and store between layers of wax paper in a tightly covered tin or dish. This halvā will keep for a week.

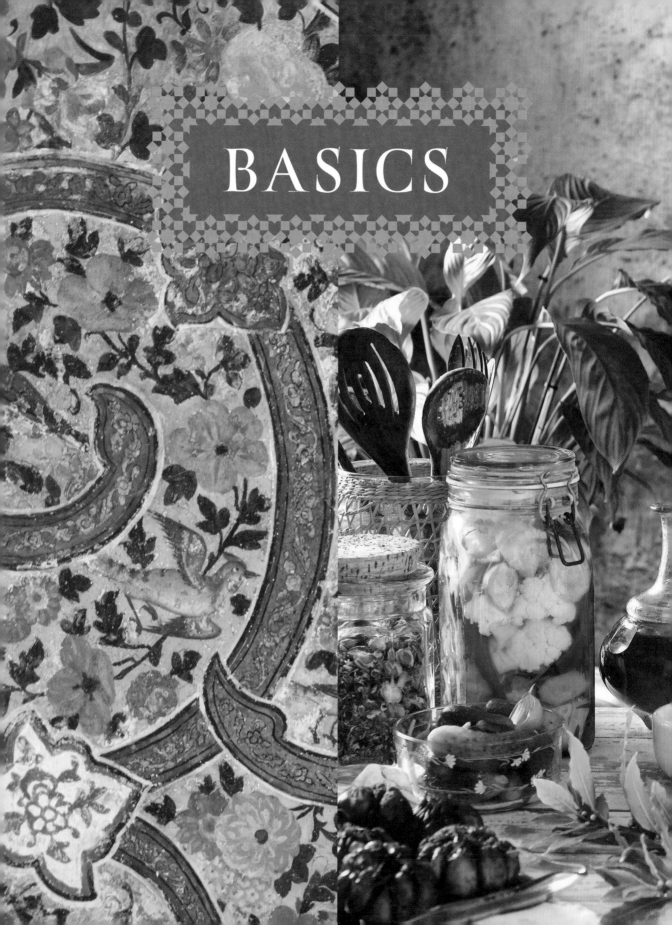

BASICS

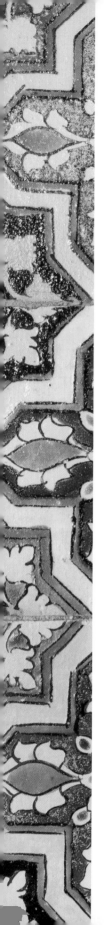

This chapter provides the basic recipes used throughout the year by Persian cooks. As such, it covers recipes for those rice dishes, meats, breads, and salads that form the backbone of our cuisine. I have also provided recipes for some of the seasonings, garnishes, pickles, and preserves that make Persian food look and taste so unique.

The Persian love affair with rice cannot be overstated. These are the six key methods for cooking rice used by every good Persian cook: Chelō (plain steamed rice); Kateh (plain rice cooked by the absorption method); Polō (traditionally refers to rice mixed with other ingredients, but now plain rice is often called polō too); Damī (rice mixed with other ingredients and cooked by the absorption method); Tahchīn (a rice cake with a golden crust, with layers of other ingredients in the middle); and Sholeh (creamy rice, whether savory or sweet).

The art of making Persian rice is not complete without the skills to make tahdīg—the crust that forms at the base of the pot and a prize worth fighting over at the dinner table. You can make your tahdīg with plain rice, or add other ingredients. The main ones used are: Flatbread (arrange a layer of thin flatbread in the oil and cover with the rice); Saffron Rice (put a little saffron water into the oil in the pot, add a few spoonfuls of the boiled rice, stir, and cover with the rest of the rice); Rice, Yogurt, Saffron (as per saffron rice above, but add a tablespoon of yogurt to the mix); Potato (arrange a layer of sliced firm-textured potatoes in the hot oil, sprinkle with salt, and then cover with the rice); Flour (mix two tablespoons flour with a pinch of salt and some water or thin yogurt to make a thick batter. Spoon into the hot oil and spread to form a thin pancake. You can add sesame, cumin, nigella, or coriander seeds to the batter for more flavor); Eggplant or Squash (cover the bottom of the pot with thick slices of eggplant or squash, making sure you keep the heat very low or the sugars will burn); Lettuce: (use two or three layers of leaves and keep the heat very low); Seeds (sprinkle a handful of sesame, sunflower, pumpkin, cumin, or coriander seeds into the oil before covering).

Rice is usually the star dish on the table, with any meat, fish, salads, or pickles served as accompaniments. Persian cooks meticulously garnish every dish they serve. In the courts of Persian kings, gold or silver leaf was strewn over food as an edible garnish. Today, fried onions, mint, and garlic are the three key garnishes.

Sprinkling any of these—or all three—over thick soups and dips enhances both the flavor and appearance. These fried garnishes can be made with any vegetable oil with a high smoking point, but not olive oil. My favorite is extra virgin canola oil.

Bread is a staple component of every meal. In Farsi, any kind of bread is called nān or nūn, and in many dialects nān (nān khordan) means having a meal. There are four main types of flatbread used throughout Iran—tāftūn, barbarī, sangak, and lavāsh. Tāftūn is probably the most popular: a thin circular loaf. Barbarī is a little thicker—more like focaccia—and comes in a long oval shape. Sangak is a wholewheat bread, but it is rarely found outside Iran, though London and Los Angeles now have bakeries serving traditional Sangak. Lavāsh is paper-thin and the hardest to make. Once dried, it can keep for several months and just needs to be sprinkled with a little water and wrapped in dish towels to soften before use. Broken matzos or Italian carta de musica are both good substitutes to add to broths.

Alongside breads, there are always a few fresh salads on the table. Iranians love fresh vegetables, but apart from our chopped tomato and cucumber salad (salad shīrāzī) and mixed herb salad (sabzī khordan) we don't have names for them. Perhaps this is because they are simple, seasonal recipes—usually a medley of garden or market vegetables with lettuce or cabbage as a base ingredient. Salads are often dressed with just a souring agent such as lemon juice, vinegar, or verjuice, though sometimes olive oil is added along with chopped fresh or dried herbs like mint, tarragon, and oregano. A number of cooked or raw vegetable dishes dressed with yogurt often appear on the table in addition to the vegetable salad.

No Persian meal is complete without at least one type of vinegary pickle (torshī). Unlike most of our food, these tend to be very hot and tart, since vinegary pickles are believed to help with digestion. Torshīs are surprisingly simple to make. The trick to making good torshī that doesn't go bad quickly is to make sure the ingredients are thoroughly dry. Pickles usually require a month or so to develop, but some of them can be eaten after a day or two.

Persian cooks make preserves, or morabbā, from everything: fruit, vegetables, citrus peel, eggplant peel, and even the green and pink skin covering fresh pistachios. Nothing is wasted. Some morabbā look like soft crystallized fruit in syrup; others are quite similar to Western jams and marmalades. Whole or chunky morabbā, particularly citrus peel, are usually served with tea at the end of a meal, presumably to help with digestion. Less chunky morabbā such as sour cherry, strawberry, carrot, rose petal, and orange blossom are favorites at the breakfast table, where they are served with clotted cream and fresh bread.

Finally, the drinks. Wine has always had a place at the Persian table. Archaeologists have found beer and wine residues in pottery jars in Iran dating from the 3rd and 4th millennium BC, respectively. Despite the Muslim conquest of Iran in 651 AD, wine continued to be made and enjoyed on a large scale. The Persian word "mey" or "may" is probably one of the most frequently used words in classical Persian poetry, while scenes depicting beautiful young men and women (known as sāghī) pouring wine for banquet guests abound in paintings and miniatures. Since the Islamic revolution of 1979, the production and consumption of alcohol has been illegal but home-made wine and distilled drinks are still enjoyed at many homes despite the high risk of serious physical punishment (lashing) or more frequently, cash fines.

A wide variety of non-alcoholic drinks including dūgh (a diluted fermented yogurt drink that is often flavored with mint or fragrant wild herbs—see page 296), flavored or plain non-alcoholic beer (mā'osha'īr), cordials (sharbat), and soft drinks are served with food in restaurants and in homes. Popular hot drinks include tea, coffee, and an array of herbal brews that are enjoyed throughout the day.

Basics

Chelō

Steamed Rice

After mounding the parboiled rice in the pot you can leave it for a couple of hours, or refrigerate for two or three days, before steaming. I usually make twice the quantity needed and keep half in a separate pot ready to steam for the next day's meal.

SERVES 4

2 cups (14 oz/400 g) white long grain rice

3 heaped tablespoons salt

2 tablespoons oil

1½ tablespoons (¾ oz/20 g) butter

½ teaspoon saffron water (page 278, optional)

Put the rice in a bowl and cover with lukewarm water. Swirl then drain off the cloudy water. Fill again with lukewarm water, and gently rub the grains between your palms. Repeat once more. Cover with enough water to come up 1½ inches (4 cm) above the rice. Add the salt and stir gently. Set aside for at least 30 minutes. The rice can be left for up to 12 hours.

Fill a medium pot with 10 cups (2½ liters) water and bring to a boil over medium heat. Drain the rice and add it to the pot. Stir once. Bring the water back to a boil and cook, uncovered, until the grains float to the surface and don't immediately sink when the heat is lowered. The rice should be soft and white but still have a little bite. Drain and rinse with lukewarm water to stop it cooking further.

Heat the oil in the same pot until very hot. Gently add the rice, mounding it in the middle. Wrap the lid in a dish towel and cover. Cook on high heat for a couple of minutes, until the side of the pot sizzles when touched with a wet finger.

Melt the butter with 2 tablespoons water and pour this over the rice. Cover the pot and lower the heat as much as you can. Let the rice steam without lifting the lid. Alternatively, place the pot in the oven at 350°F (180°C) for 30–45 minutes.

Approximately 30 minutes after the first signs of steam appear, gently tap the mound. It will "tremble" a little if it's done. Transfer the rice to a platter. Put a few tablespoons of the rice in a bowl and add the saffron water. Top the mound with the saffron rice. Lift the crispy rice (tahdīg) from the bottom of the pot and serve on a separate plate or arrange around the rice on the platter.

Kateh

Steamed Rice

This method uses a ratio of 1¾ measures of water for every 1 measure of rice. The easiest way to do this is in cups—be it a measuring cup, or any cup from your shelf. What is important is the proportion of wet to dry. In dry climates, like Iran, a little more water is sometimes needed, but this is a good standard measure for most places. Make sure you lower the heat as much as you can after the water is absorbed, or use a heat diffuser. The amount of oil you use is up to you. More oil makes fluffier rice and a crispier tahdīg (crust).

SERVES 4–6

2 cups (14 oz/400 g) long grain rice

3½ cups (830 ml) water

1 teaspoon salt

3 tablespoons canola or other vegetable oil

1½ tablespoons (¾ oz/20 g) butter

Put the rice in a nonstick pot, around 8 inches (20 cm) in diameter. Fill with cold water and swirl it around. Pour off the cloudy water and fill the pot again. Gently rub the rice between your palms, then stir and drain again. Repeat until the water is clear (two or three times in total). Add the measured water, salt, and oil. You can leave the rice to soak for an hour or two before cooking (this helps to separate the grains, but is not essential).

To cook the rice, stir it gently, and then bring to a boil over medium-high heat on the medium burner of your stovetop. When all the water is absorbed, lower the heat to medium-low. Wrap the lid of the pot in a clean dish towel and cover the pot tightly. Let the rice steam for 30–45 minutes, depending on how browned you want your tahdīg. Kateh is ready when the rice around the side of the pot is a little crispy and beginning to color.

When you are almost ready to serve, dot the top of the kateh with pats of butter, cover the pot, and steam for about 5 minutes, then put a flat plate on the top of the pot and, holding tightly with both hands, invert the rice onto the plate. Serve immediately.

Morgh-e Zaferānī
Saffron Braised Chicken

This braised chicken recipe from my mother-in-law is a favorite with almost any kind of rice, but particularly zereshk polō (page 156).

SERVES 4–6

3 tablespoons oil

3 lb (1.3 kg) bone-in chicken thighs or breasts, or a mixture

2 onions, finely chopped

½ teaspoon ground turmeric

¼ teaspoon whole cumin seeds

2 cloves of garlic, peeled

1 teaspoon salt

2 cups (500 ml) boiling water

3 carrots, sliced

Salt and black pepper

1–2 teaspoons saffron water (page 278)

Pat of butter

1 tablespoon barberries, to garnish (optional)

Parsley sprigs, to garnish (optional)

Heat the oil in a deep frying pan over medium heat and fry the chicken pieces until golden on both sides. Remove and set aside. Add the chopped onions and sauté until almost golden. Sprinkle over the turmeric and cumin and cook for another minute or two. Add the garlic cloves, salt, and boiling water, then return the chicken to the pan with any juices. Add the carrots and bring to a boil, then lower the heat and simmer, covered, for 30 minutes.

Taste and add salt and pepper, if necessary. If the sauce has reduced too much, add a little hot water from the kettle. Add the saffron water and turn the chicken pieces over, then cover the pan and cook for 10–15 minutes until very tender.

Melt the butter in a small saucepan and add the barberries. Cook over medium-low heat for a minute or two until shiny and puffed up. Sprinkle them over the chicken, garnish with parsley if you wish, and serve with your choice of rice.

Khorāk-e Morgh
Braised Chicken in Tomato Sauce

Eat this with reshteh polō (page 205), bāghālī polō (page 34), or just plain steamed rice.

SERVES 4–6

3 tablespoons oil

3 lb (1.3 kg) bone-in chicken legs or breasts, or a mixture

2 onions, finely chopped

1 teaspoon ground turmeric

1 teaspoon salt

1 teaspoon whole peppercorns

3–4 cloves of garlic, peeled

5 tablespoons tomato paste

2 cups (500 ml) boiling water

Lemon, lime, sour orange juice, or verjuice, to taste

1 quantity shallow-fried potatoes (page 281)

Parsley leaves, to garnish (optional)

Heat the oil in a deep frying pan over medium heat and fry the chicken pieces until golden on both sides. Remove and set aside. Add the chopped onions and sauté until golden. Sprinkle over the turmeric and cook for another minute or two. Add the salt, peppercorns, garlic cloves, and tomato paste and cook for 2 minutes, stirring all the time. Pour over the water and return the chicken to the pan with any juices. Bring to a boil, then lower the heat and simmer, covered, for 30 minutes or until the chicken is tender.

If the sauce has reduced too much, add a little more hot water from the kettle. Taste and add as much lemon juice or other souring agent as you like. Cover and cook for 10–20 minutes or until the chicken pieces are meltingly tender. Remove the peppercorns and garlic if you wish, garnish with parsley, and serve with some shallow-fried potatoes.

Khorāk-e Māhīcheh

Braised Lamb Shanks

This recipe is a modern version of yakhnī—meat cooked in broth. In medieval times, yakhnī shops sold pre-cooked meat to those who couldn't afford the fuel for the long, slow braising required. This recipe works nicely with other cuts of lamb or mutton, as well as beef shin and even goat. For saffron lamb shanks, skip the tomato paste and add a little saffron water (page 278) towards the end of cooking.

SERVES 4

3 tablespoons oil

4 lamb shanks

1 teaspoon ground turmeric

2 onions, finely chopped

1 teaspoon salt, plus more if needed

4 cloves of garlic, peeled

2 tablespoons tomato paste (optional)

1–2 bay leaves

1 tablespoon whole peppercorns

1 cinnamon stick

½ teaspoon whole cumin seeds

Fresh herbs, to garnish (optional)

1 quantity shallow-fried potatoes (page 281, optional)

Heat the oil in a large heavy-bottomed Dutch oven over medium heat and brown the shanks on all sides. Sprinkle over the turmeric and cook for a minute or two. Remove the meat from the pot and set aside. Add the chopped onions and fry until golden. Add the salt, garlic cloves, tomato paste, bay leaves, and spices and cook for a minute or two. Return the shanks to the pot and pour in enough water to just cover. Bring to a boil, then lower the heat and simmer gently for 2½ –3 hours, or until the meat is almost falling off the bone. Remove the shanks and set aside.

Reduce the broth until you have just over 1 cup (about 300ml) left. Pass the broth through a sieve, then return it to the pot along with the shanks. Season with salt, if needed, and cook over low heat for another 10 minutes. Garnish with herbs and serve with shallow-fried potatoes or rice.

Tāftūn

Flatbread

Tāftūn is similar to Indian naan, but slightly thinner and lighter. They keep well in the freezer—all they need are a few seconds in a warm oven or toaster to soften. You can add a whole variety of seeds or spices to your mix: my favorites are sesame seeds (both black and white) and nigella seeds.

MAKES 6-8 FLATBREADS

4 cups (1 lb/500 g) all-purpose flour, plus more for flouring

1½ teaspoons salt

1 envelope (¼ oz/7g) instant yeast

½ tablespoon sugar

1 cup (250 ml) milk

⅔ cup (150 ml) plain yogurt, at room temperature

2 tablespoons oil, plus more for greasing

Seeds, for sprinkling (optional)

Put the flour, salt, yeast, and sugar in a large bowl and stir well to combine. Gently heat the milk until it's a little warmer than your finger. Put the yogurt and oil in a jug, then gradually add the milk and stir well.

Make a well in the center of the flour and add the warm liquid. Stir gently with a wooden spoon to create a dough. If it's too sticky, add a small amount of flour, or a little more milk if it's too stiff. The dough should be very soft, so stop adding flour as soon as it doesn't stick to your hands anymore. Turn it out onto a floured surface and knead for 10 minutes, then place in a lightly greased bowl. Cover and leave to rise in a warm place for 2–3 hours, until more than doubled in size.

Punch the dough down and shape into 2 inch (5 cm) balls (or larger if you want). Put the balls on a lightly floured surface and cover with a dish towel. Leave to rest for about 30 minutes.

Using a floured rolling pin, roll a ball of dough into a very thin circle. Sprinkle with your favorite seeds, if using, then roll again to incorporate. Using a small knife, make several small incisions in the dough. Put a heavy-bottomed frying pan or griddle (without ridges) on the largest burner on your stovetop. Heat over high until very hot, then reduce the heat to medium. Drop the dough into the hot pan and start rolling out the next piece while the first cooks.

Flip the bread over once it's risen slightly and the bottom is speckled with brown. Cook for a couple of minutes until speckled with brown on the other side too. Remove from the pan and allow to cool on a rack. Repeat with the rest of the dough. Stack and wrap the cooled bread in a clean towel until required. Warm in a medium oven briefly before serving.

Barbarī

Flatbread

Barbarī is great for breakfast with butter or clotted cream and honey or jam; with cucumbers, cheese, tomatoes, and herbs as a snack; or as a scoop for omlet (page 94), mīrza ghāsemī (page 90), and a myriad of other dips. It freezes very well, so make a bigger batch and save some in the freezer for later use.

MAKES 2 LOAVES

4 cups (1¼ lb/550 g) white bread flour

2 teaspoons salt

1 tablespoon instant yeast

1¾ cups (400 ml) warm water

Fine cornmeal or bran

Sesame or nigella seeds, for sprinkling

Oil, for greasing

FOR THE GLAZE

1 teaspoon all-purpose flour

1 teaspoon baking soda

⅔ cup (150 ml) cold water

In a large bowl combine the flour, salt, and yeast. Make a well in the middle and pour in the warm water. Gradually draw the flour to the center and mix until a soft, sticky dough forms. Turn the dough out onto a floured surface and form into a ball with lightly floured hands. Knead the dough for about 8 minutes until elastic. Don't add too much flour or it will be hard to shape later. Place in a lightly oiled bowl and cover. Leave in a warm place to rise for about 1 hour or until doubled in size.

Put the ingredients for the glaze in a small saucepan. Bring to a boil over low heat, stirring all the time, and continue stirring until thickened. Punch down the dough and divide it into two balls. Cover and leave to stand for another 20 minutes. Preheat the oven to its highest setting. Place two baking sheets in the oven to heat through. Cut two pieces of parchment paper the size of the baking sheets and lightly dust with cornmeal or bran.

Gently punch the air out of the dough balls. Put one ball on a lightly floured surface and shape into an oval, then roll out until the dough is about ¼ inch (½ cm) thick. Place the loaf on the parchment paper and neaten the shape. With the handle of a wooden spoon or the tips of your fingers, make deep parallel ridges ¾ inch (2 cm) apart along the loaf, pressing about halfway through the loaf. Spoon 2 tablespoons of the glaze over the loaf and spread with your hand to cover the entire surface. Sprinkle liberally with the seeds. Repeat with the other ball.

Remove the baking sheets from the oven and place the parchment paper containing the loaves on them. Place both in the oven and bake for about 20 minutes or until golden. Remove from the oven and allow to cool for 10 minutes before serving.

Sālād Shīrāzī
Chopped Tomato and Cucumber Salad

Like Mexican pico de gallo and kachumbari in some African cuisines, sālād shīrāzī is often used like a condiment, spooned over rice and other main dishes. Persian or Lebanese cucumbers have a more intense flavor and thinner skin than the large English cucumbers. Use them if you can find them.

SERVES 4

¾ English cucumber, or
3 Persian or Lebanese cucumbers

4 firm tomatoes

1 small onion (optional)

2 mild chili peppers (optional)

1 teaspoon dried mint (optional)

Pomegranate seeds (optional)

Souring agent (lime or lemon juice, verjuice, or wine vinegar)

Olive oil (optional)

Sea salt and black pepper, to taste

Peel the cucumber if the skin is leathery. Dice the cucumber and put it in a bowl. Dice the tomatoes and drain well in a sieve—too much juice will dilute the dressing. Dice the onion and slice the chilies, if using. Sprinkle the mint and pomegranate seeds (if using) over the vegetables and toss. Make a dressing with your preferred souring agent and olive oil, if using. Just before serving, pour the dressing over the salad, season with salt and pepper, and toss.

Māst Khiyār
Yogurt and Cucumber Salad

This is a particularly good accompaniment to rich pilafs such as lūbiyā polō (page 36).

SERVES 4

1 cup (250 ml) Greek yogurt

1 English cucumber, or 3 Persian or Lebanese cucumbers, diced or grated

1 small clove of garlic, grated

1 tablespoon dried mint, crushed

Salt, to taste

Combine all of the ingredients and mix well.

Māst Khiyār-e Majlesī
Garnished Yogurt and Cucumber Salad

A fancy version of māst khiyār—the "majlesī" in the name means, "for banquets."

SERVES 4

2 tablespoons dried rose petals

¼ cup (1 oz/30 g) coarsely chopped walnuts

¼ cup (1 oz/30 g) currants

1 cup (250 ml) Greek or strained yogurt (page 255)

1 small English cucumber, or 3 Persian or Lebanese cucumbers, diced

1 tablespoon dried mint, crushed

1 tablespoon dried dill, crushed

½ tablespoon dried summer savory or thyme, crushed

Pinch of garlic powder

Sea salt and white pepper

Reserve some rose petals, walnuts, currants, dried herbs, and diced cucumber for garnishing. Crush the rest of the rose petals between your palms—heating them in a dry pan for a few seconds will make this easier—and mix with the dried herbs.

Combine the yogurt, with the remaining diced cucumber, walnuts, currants, dried herbs, and the garlic powder and mix well. Taste and season with salt and pepper. If you are using strained yogurt and it's too thick, just add a little water or regular yogurt to soften it to your liking. Leave in the fridge for a couple of hours for the flavors to meld and the currants to soften a bit. This will keep in the fridge for a day.

When ready to serve, decorate with the reserved ingredients and eat with toasted flatbread.

Būrānī-ye Esfenāj
Wilted Spinach, Yogurt, and Walnut Salad

This is delicious to have on the table when spinach is in season. It can be eaten on its own but is even better with warmed flatbread.

SERVES 4

1¾ lb (800 g) fresh spinach, washed and coarsely chopped if leaves are large

1¾ cups (400 ml) Greek or strained yogurt (recipe below)

½ cup (1¾ oz/50 g) walnuts, chopped

½ teaspoon salt

½ teaspoon ground white pepper

2–3 cloves of garlic, very finely mashed or grated (optional)

½ teaspoon saffron water (page 278)

Put the spinach in a saucepan with the water clinging to it from washing (or 2 tablespoons water if it comes pre-washed). Cover and cook for 5 minutes over medium-low heat, until the leaves are wilted. Drain well, pressing with a spoon to extract as much water as you can.

Save a couple of spoonfuls of the yogurt and a few pieces of walnuts for garnishing. In a bowl, combine the rest of the yogurt, walnuts, salt, white pepper, and garlic, then stir in the spinach. Put it in a bowl and allow the flavors to combine for a couple of hours. Garnish with the reserved yogurt and walnut pieces and drizzle the saffron water on top.

Māst-e Chekīdeh
Strained Yogurt

This strained yogurt is very thick, almost like a cream cheese. It will keep in the fridge for a couple of weeks. Use live culture yogurt so it ferments a little and develops its characteristic tangy flavor.

MAKES ABOUT 1 CUP (250 ML)

Pinch of sea salt

3 cups (750 ml) live culture yogurt

Line a sieve or colander with several layers of cheesecloth or a clean dish towel and place over a bowl. Add the sea salt to the yogurt, then pour into the lined sieve. Cover with the edges of the cheesecloth or dish towel and leave to drain for several hours or overnight, stirring two or three times, until the yogurt is very thick, and easily separates from the cloth when tilted. Place in a clean, airtight container and store in the fridge.

Būrānī-ye Bādemjūn
Eggplant and Yogurt Salad

Legend has it that this dish was named after Būrān, the beloved Persian wife of the ninth-century caliph of Baghdad, and was created for her extravagant wedding feast. This dish is often made with mashed chargrilled eggplant. For chargrilling instructions please see the recipe for kāl kabāb, page 258.

SERVES 4

⅓ cup (80 ml) oil

3 medium eggplants, peeled and cubed

1¼ cups (300 ml) Greek yogurt

1 large clove of garlic, finely mashed or grated

½ teaspoon salt

½ teaspoon ground white pepper

½ cup (1¾ oz/50 g) walnuts, chopped

A few drops of saffron water (page 278)

Heat the oil in a large nonstick frying pan and add the eggplant. Cover with a lid and cook over medium heat, stirring from time to time, until golden brown.

Mix the yogurt with the garlic, salt, and pepper. Reserve a couple of tablespoons of the chopped walnuts and a few cubes of eggplant for the garnish and stir the rest into the yogurt.

Turn the mixture into a serving dish and garnish with the reserved walnuts, eggplants, and the saffron water if you wish. Serve with warm flatbread.

Kāl Kabāb

Smoky Eggplant Salad with Walnuts

Kāl kabāb is usually served as a side dish or eaten with rice and salted fish. It would also go nicely with the recipe for northern-style stuffed fish (page 10).

SERVES 4

2 large eggplants

1 pomegranate

¼ cup (1 oz/30 g) walnuts

3 tablespoons extra-virgin olive oil

A handful of mint leaves, finely chopped

A handful of cilantro leaves, finely chopped

2 cloves of garlic, grated

Small pinch of golpar (optional)

Verjuice or fresh lemon juice

Salt and black pepper

A few mint leaves, to garnish

Make a shallow lengthways cut on each eggplant, then grill in a medium-hot barbecue until the skin is charred and the flesh is very soft. Alternatively, bake them in an oven preheated to 475°F (240°C) for about 45 minutes. Leave to cool a little, then split open along the cut and scoop out the flesh. Mash the pulp and leave to drain in a sieve for at least 10 minutes.

Remove the seeds from the pomegranate. Put a handful aside and crush the rest of the seeds in a mortar and pestle. Place in a sieve and drain over a bowl to catch the juice. Press with the back of a spoon to extract as much juice as you can. Discard the pulp. Pound the walnuts to a very coarse paste in the mortar and pestle.

Mix the eggplant pulp with the pomegranate juice, oil, walnuts, chopped herbs, garlic, and golpar. Flavor with as much verjuice or lemon juice as you wish and season with salt and black pepper to taste. Turn the mixture into a bowl and garnish with the reserved pomegranate seeds and a few mint leaves. Serve at room temperature.

Zeytūn Parvardeh
Walnut and Pomegranate Olives

Served with lightly toasted flatbread, these marinated olives make a tasty appetizer but, like most of the dishes in this section, they are just "mokhallafāt" for us—that is to say, "other things," to be eaten alongside main dishes.

SERVES 4

1 cup (3½ oz/100 g) walnuts

¼ cup (60 ml) extra-virgin olive oil

¼ cup (60 ml) pomegranate molasses

1 tablespoon dried mint

½ cup (1 oz/30 g) cilantro leaves

¼ teaspoon black pepper

1 garlic clove, finely mashed or grated

Salt, to taste

Lemon juice

9 oz (250 g) pitted green olives

3 tablespoons pomegranate seeds (optional)

Put half of the walnuts in a food processor along with the oil, pomegranate molasses, dried mint, cilantro, and black pepper. Pulse until finely chopped. Add the rest of the walnuts, along with the garlic and salt and pulse for a few seconds, leaving a bit of texture in the marinade. Adjust the sweet-sour flavor balance to your liking by adding some lemon juice.

Mix the olives with the marinade and refrigerate for a minimum of 2 hours. A day or two in the fridge will improve the flavors greatly. Sprinkle with pomegranate seeds and serve.

Torshī Makhlūt
Mixed Vegetable Pickles

You can chop the vegetables for this as large or as small as you wish. This will keep for weeks in the refrigerator. Mūsīr (sometimes sold as Persian shallots) can be found in Iranian grocery stores or online.

MAKES 2–3 PINT (16 OZ) JARS

1¾ oz (50 g) dried sliced mūsīr (optional)

2 tender stems of celery

2 carrots

½ red pepper

½ green pepper

1 red chili pepper

4 cauliflower florets

3 cloves of garlic

1 teaspoon coriander seeds, lightly crushed

1 teaspoon ground turmeric

½ teaspoon nigella seeds

½ teaspoon ground cumin

1 teaspoon ground golpar (optional)

1 tablespoon salt

2 tablespoons tomato paste

White wine vinegar with at least 5% acidity

Put the mūsīr in a glass or ceramic bowl and cover with plenty of cold water. Change the water two or three times until the slices are completely reconstituted. Rinse, drain, and spread on paper towels to dry. Wash the vegetables and leave to dry for a few hours.

Chop the vegetables and mūsīr into bite-sized pieces and combine with the garlic, spices, salt, and tomato paste in a clean bowl. Prepare two or three medium-sized jars with vinegar-safe lids by washing them thoroughly, then allowing them to air-dry. Once cool, fill the jars with the vegetable mixture and top up with white wine vinegar. Refrigerate for at least 2 weeks to develop.

Torshī Mashhadī
Tomato and Cauliflower Pickle

This condiment has less vinegar so it will keep better if your jars are sterilized. To sterilize, place your jars in a large pot and fully submerge with water. Bring to a boil and boil for 10 minutes. These pickles can be enjoyed after developing for a week or so and will keep for a few weeks in the fridge. If you want to speed up the process, bring the mixture to a boil quickly before filling your jars. This will help the flavors develop faster.

MAKES 2–3 PINT
(16 OZ) JARS

2 carrots

1 small head of cauliflower

4 stalks of celery

6 cloves of garlic

3 red chili peppers

1 tablespoon salt

1 tablespoon ground coriander

½ tablespoon ground turmeric

2 cups (500 ml) tomato juice or passata

⅔ cup (150ml) white wine vinegar

Wash the vegetables and leave to dry for a few hours. Chop into bite-sized pieces and slice the garlic and chilies. Mix the chopped vegetables, salt, and spices in a bowl. Add the tomato juice and vinegar then pour into sterilized jars. Make sure the liquid is cool before covering the jars and storing in the refrigerator.

Torshī Anbeh
Baluchi Mango Relish

This spicy torshī comes from the southern regions of Sistan and Baluchestan. Baluchi women make this relish with baby mangoes, leaving the chopped fruit out in the scorching sun to dehydrate for a few hours before mixing with the other ingredients. The following method doesn't require scorching sunshine, but it does benefit from sitting in the refrigerator for a week or so. Very unripe mangoes often found in supermarkets work nicely in this recipe. Serve with shāmi (page 22) and southern-style dishes like Chabahari fish stew (page 182).

**MAKES 1 SMALL
(12 OZ) JAR**

1 large unripe mango, peeled and thinly sliced

1 tablespoon crushed sea salt

2 tablespoons ground turmeric

¼ cup (60 ml) oil

½ teaspoon ground cumin

½ teaspoon garlic powder

½ teaspoon ground black pepper

2 teaspoons nigella seeds

1 heaped teaspoon cayenne pepper, or to taste

1 tablespoon white wine vinegar

Sprinkle the mango with the sea salt and turmeric and toss well. Leave to stand for 1 hour while the mango slices release some of their juices, then place in a small saucepan and cook over medium-low heat, stirring all the time, until the mango breaks down. You can add 1 tablespoon of hot water to help cook the mango faster, but make sure the water evaporates completely.

Heat the oil in a medium saucepan and add the cumin, garlic powder, black pepper, nigella seeds, and cayenne. Cook for 1 minute, then turn off the heat and allow to cool. Mix the spiced oil with the vinegar then pour over the mango and mix well. Pour into a clean jar, allow to cool before covering, and store in the refrigerator. Use within a few weeks.

Līteh Bādemjūn

Herby Eggplant Pickle

This torshī is particularly nice with ābgūsht-e sabzī (page 18) and shāmī-ye bāboli (page 22), or kotlet (page 21). It can be enjoyed right away, but it tastes even better after a couple of weeks. It will keep for a few weeks in the fridge.

**MAKES 2 SMALL
(12 OZ) JARS**

1 carrot

3 cauliflower florets

½ red bell pepper

⅓ cup (¾ oz/20 g) tarragon

⅓ cup (¾ oz/20 g) parsley

⅔ cup (1½ oz/40 g) mint

⅔ cup (1½ oz/40 g) cilantro

1 large eggplant

2 cloves of garlic

1–2 red chili peppers

2 teaspoons nigella seeds

½ teaspoon cayenne pepper

1 teaspoon ground coriander

1 teaspoon ground cumin

½ teaspoon ground celery seeds

1 tablespoon ground turmeric

Scant ½ cup (100 ml) tomato passata, purée, or juice

1 tablespoon salt

White wine vinegar

Wash the carrot, cauliflower, bell pepper, and herbs and leave to dry for a few hours.

Preheat the oven to 425°F (220°C). Prick the eggplant all over with a fork and bake in the oven for 30 minutes or until soft and charred. Leave to cool. Cut the eggplant in half and scoop out the flesh. Mash well and leave to drain in a sieve.

Finely chop the vegetables, herbs, garlic, and chili peppers. Mix together the drained eggplant pulp, chopped vegetables, herbs, spices, passata, and salt. Add enough white wine vinegar to make a thin paste. Store in clean jars in the refrigerator.

Sīr Torshī

Aged Garlic Pickles

This is ready to eat after six months but if you can't wait, cook the garlic in vinegar briefly, then cover with fresh vinegar and refrigerate. This way, the pickle can be eaten after a month. Like balsamic vinegar, the longer this sits, the more prized it will be. See page 264 for sterilizing instructions.

MAKES 1 LARGE
(32 OZ) JAR

10–12 bulbs of garlic, unpeeled
1 teaspoon sea salt flakes
2–3 tablespoons sugar
Small handful of barberries (optional)
Red wine vinegar with 5% acidity

Peel one layer of the papery skin from the garlic heads. Place in a sterilized wide-mouthed jar, along with the salt, sugar, and barberries (if using) and then fully cover with vinegar. Shake the jar to dissolve the salt and sugar. Leave in a cool, dark place for a few months.

Torshī-ye Holū

Peach Pickle

This makes a good accompaniment to rich stews and is best made with unripe peaches.

MAKES 2 SMALL
(12 OZ) JARS

3 peaches
1 small carrot
½ red pepper
3 cauliflower florets
1½ teaspoons nigella seeds
½ teaspoon ground turmeric
½ teaspoon cayenne pepper
½ teaspoon ground cumin
1 teaspoon ground coriander
1 teaspoon ground golpar
½ teaspoon garlic powder
2 tablespoons sugar
1 teaspoon salt
1 cup plus 1 tablespoon (260 ml) white wine vinegar

Peel the peaches and carrot, then finely dice them, along with the red pepper. Break the cauliflower into small pieces. Put all the ingredients in a non-reactive saucepan. Bring to a boil and turn off the heat. Pour into clean jars, allow to cool fully, and cover. Refrigerate for at least a week before using, to allow the flavors to develop.

Shūr
Fermented Vegetable Pickle

My mom made huge amounts of this every fall, when cauliflowers are at their best. Adding a couple of dried chickpeas to each jar is supposed to help with the fermentation process and keep the veggies even crisper.

MAKES 2-3 LARGE
(32 OZ) JARS
1 medium head of cauliflower
½ red pepper
2 carrots
¼ small head white cabbage
2 stalks celery
⅓ cup (¾ oz/20 g) dill
2½ tablespoons cilantro
⅓ cup (¾ oz/20 g) tarragon
1 small bay leaf for each jar
A few unpeeled cloves of garlic
A few red chili peppers
A few dried chickpeas (optional)
8 cups (2 liters) water
3½ oz (100 g) sea salt
⅔ cup (150ml) white wine vinegar

Wash and dry all the vegetables thoroughly before cutting into evenly sized pieces. Pack the vegetables into sterilized jars, layering them with the herbs, garlic, and chili peppers. Add a couple of uncooked chickpeas to each jar.

To make the brine, bring the water to a boil in a clean pot (any trace of oil may spoil your pickle). Add the salt and vinegar and boil for 1 minute, then immediately pour over the vegetables. Screw on the lids and turn the jars upside down. Leave to cool.

Put the jars on a tray, right side up, and check every day. When the lids start to swell and gas begins to rise from the bottom of the jars, loosen the lids a bit so they don't burst. The brine may become quite cloudy at first but will clear later. When the brine is clear and the bubbling has come to an end, tighten the lids again and store in the refrigerator. Alternatively, you can use special fermentation jars, now available online and in stores, that are fitted with valves to allow the gas to escape during fermentation. Wait for 2 or 3 weeks before enjoying the pickles. Shūr will keep for months in the refrigerator.

Khiyār Shūr
Fermented Cucumber Pickles

These are most likely of Polish origin. During World War II, more than a hundred thousand Polish refugees ended up in Iran having travelled on foot through Russia. Many of them settled permanently, and these brined, fermented cucumbers are just one of their lovely contributions to our modern cuisine. Use the smallest Middle Eastern cucumbers you can find or pickling gherkins—this recipe will not work with large cucumbers as they are too watery. Adjust the amount of chili and garlic to your taste but never skip the herbs—that's where the flavor lies.

MAKES 2-3 PINT
(16 OZ) JARS
⅓ cup (¾ oz/20 g) dill
2½ tablespoons cilantro
⅓ cup (¾ oz/20 g) tarragon
2¼ lb (1 kg) small Persian or Lebanese cucumbers
A few chili peppers
A few cloves of garlic, unpeeled
A few dried chickpeas (optional)
8 cups (2 liters) water
⅓ cup (3½ oz/100 g) salt
⅔ cup (150ml) white wine vinegar

Wash the herbs and leave to dry for a couple of hours. Pack the whole cucumbers, herbs, chilies, and garlic cloves into sterilized jars. Add a few dried chickpeas to each jar.

To make the brine, bring the water to a boil in a very clean pot (any trace of oil may spoil your pickles). Add the salt and vinegar and boil for 1 minute. Allow the brine to cool for a couple of minutes, then pour over the cucumbers. Screw on the lids and turn the jars upside down. Leave to cool.

Put the jars on a tray on the counter, right way up, and check every day. When the lids start to swell and gas begins to rise from the bottom of the jars, loosen the lids. Tighten the lids again when the brine is clear and the bubbling has stopped, and store the jars in the refrigerator. Alternatively, use special fermentation jars now available online and in shops. Wait for 2 or 3 weeks before enjoying your pickles.

Piyāz Dāgh
Fried Onions

MAKES 4 PORTIONS
Oil, for frying
4 small onions, thinly sliced
Pinch of salt
½ teaspoon ground turmeric

Pour the oil into a medium frying pan to a depth of 1½ inches (4 cm). Heat over medium-low, then add the sliced onions and a pinch of salt. Cook for 15 minutes, or until they are golden brown, then add the turmeric and cook for another couple of minutes. Remove with a slotted spoon and divide into four portions. Cover, and store in the fridge for up to a week, or the freezer for 2 months.

Na'nā Dāgh
Fried Mint

2 heaped tablespoons dried mint
Oil, for frying

Rub the dried mint between your palms to create a rough powder. Heat a small saucepan over medium heat and add a few big glugs of oil. When the oil is hot, lower the heat and add the mint. Cook, stirring, for a few seconds or until the mint is fragrant and the oil takes on a greenish color. Remove from the heat immediately to avoid burning the mint.

Sīr Dāgh
Fried Garlic

Oil, for frying
5 cloves of garlic, thinly sliced

Place a small saucepan over medium heat and add a few big glugs of oil. Once hot, add the garlic and cook until the slices begin to turn golden. Stir from time to time to color them evenly. Remove from the heat and keep stirring until the oil is no longer hot. Be careful not to burn the garlic.

Zafarān

Saffron Water

Persian cooks use saffron in their dishes on a daily basis, lending its distinctive golden color to every mealtime. It is usually added to food in the form of saffron water, a red liquid obtained by infusing the powdered threads in water.

Large pinch of saffron threads
1 tablespoon very hot (nearly boiling) water

Grind the saffron threads with a mortar and pestle. If they aren't quite dry enough, place in a warm pan off the heat for a few minutes to dry out.

In a small jar, steep the ground saffron in the very hot water. Place in a warm place (near the stove for example) to infuse for a few minutes. If your saffron is of good quality, ¼ teaspoon of the liquid and its sediment will be enough to color and flavor a whole dish. Saffron water keeps well in the fridge for a week or two.

Sīb Zamīnī Sorkh Kardeh

Shallow-Fried Potatoes

We like our potatoes golden and crispy almost all the way through, unlike French fries that are soft inside. To make the crispiest of fries it is important to choose firm floury potatoes such as russets.

SERVES 4

3 firm potatoes, peeled and cut into sticks, cubes, or shoestrings
2 tablespoons table salt
Oil, for frying
Very small pinch of ground turmeric (optional)
Sea salt, for sprinkling (optional)

Wash and rinse the potato sticks, then place in a bowl and cover with cold water. Add salt and stir well. Leave to stand for an hour or so. Drain and spread over a clean dish towel to dry.

Heat 1½ inches (4 cm) of oil in a large nonstick frying pan over high heat until the oil is very hot but not smoking (about 350°F/180°C). Drop the potatoes into the oil in three batches, 30 seconds apart, so that the temperature doesn't drop. Thirty seconds after the last batch goes in, stir once then lower the heat to medium. If your pan is small, fry the potatoes in two batches. There should only be one layer in the pan at a time while frying.

Wait until the undersides of the potato sticks begin to color, then gently turn them over and fry the other side. Be careful though; stirring too soon will make them mushy. Once the potatoes are lightly golden, sprinkle the turmeric in the oil and stir the potatoes for 2 minutes or until golden. Transfer to a plate lined with paper towels to drain and sprinkle with coarse sea salt if desired.

Sar Gonjeshkī
Tiny Meatballs

Many Persian recipes use these tiny fried meatballs either as a garnish or within the dish itself. I sometimes use them as a substitute for meat in stews such as khoresht-e gheymeh (page 187) since it considerably reduces the cooking time and is just as delicious.

SERVES 4

14 oz (400 g) lean ground lamb or beef
¾ teaspoon ground turmeric
½ teaspoon mild curry powder
½ teaspoon salt
¼ teaspoon black pepper
1 onion, grated
1 tablespoon oil

Combine the meat, turmeric, curry powder, salt, pepper, and onion. Shape the mixture into small meatballs, around the size of a cherry tomato.

Heat the oil over medium heat and fry the meatballs until lightly brown all over. Remove with a slotted spoon and use as directed in your recipe.

Morabbā-ye Kadū Halvāyī
Preserved Squash

This delicious sweet preserve takes time, but is worth it. I have provided two methods: my mom's takes longer, but keeps the squash very crunchy. My method is speedier, although the resulting preserve is not as crunchy.

MAKES 2 SMALL (12 OZ) JARS
10½ oz (300 g) pickling lime (for my mom's method)
1 lb (500 g) butternut squash, peeled and seeds removed
2½ cups (1 lb/500 g) sugar
1 tablespoon fresh lemon juice

My mother's method: put the pickling lime in a large glass bowl and add 4 cups (1 liter) of water. Stir well and allow the lime to settle for a few minutes. Pour the lime solution into another glass bowl and discard the sediment.

Cut the squash however you like, but the pieces can't be too thick or else the lime solution won't penetrate them. Add the squash to the lime solution and leave for 24 hours. Drain well and rinse under running water. Soak in plenty of water for 4 hours. Drain, rinse, and repeat three more times.

Put the sugar and 2 cups (500 ml) of water into a saucepan and bring to a boil. Add the drained squash and turn the heat very low. Cook for 40 minutes or until the syrup is as thick as runny honey. Add the lemon juice and cook for 5 minutes. Remove from the heat and pour into sterilized jars while still hot. Allow to cool before covering. This will keep in the fridge for a few weeks.

My speedier method: cut the squash into pieces. Bring the sugar and 2 cups (500 ml) water to a boil. Cook for about 10 minutes over low heat or until the syrup is the consistency of honey. Add the squash and stir. Cook over low for 10 minutes. Turn off the heat and leave to stand for a few hours. The squash will release some of its water and dilute the syrup.

Remove the squash and set aside. Bring the syrup back to a boil and reduce, again, to the consistency of honey. Return the squash to the syrup, turn off the heat, and leave for a couple of hours. Repeat one more time or until the syrup lightly coats the back of a spoon. Add the lemon juice and bring to a boil. Remove from the heat and pour into sterilized jars. Allow to cool before covering and storing in the refrigerator.

Morabbā-ye Kāmkuāt
Preserved Kumquats

Kumquats were introduced to the Caspian Sea region around thirty years ago. Though they were initially a novelty, it didn't take long for Iranian cooks to discover kumquats' great potential for making preserves. If you find them too bitter, cook them in plenty of cold water for about ten minutes before starting step one of the method below.

MAKES 2 SMALL
(12 OZ) JARS
12 oz (350 g) kumquats
1¼ cups (9 oz/250 g) sugar
⅓ cup (2½ oz/70 g) gelling sugar
(or use regular sugar)
1¾ cups (400 ml) water
2 tablespoons fresh lemon juice

Make three deep intersecting cuts at one end of each kumquat going two-thirds of the way down. Remove the pits with a wooden skewer. Put the kumquats in a small saucepan and mix with the sugars. Allow to stand for 1 hour.

Pour over the water and bring to a boil over medium-low heat. Cook for 15 minutes, or until the kumquats are soft. Remove the kumquats with a slotted spoon and set aside. Continue to cook the syrup until it is as thick as honey. Add the lemon juice, return the kumquats to the pan, and cook for a further 5 minutes. Place in small sterilized jars, allow to cool fully, and cover. Store in the refrigerator and use within a few weeks.

Morabbā-ye Beh
Quince Jam

Come quince season, people all across Iran make this delicious jam. With long cooking, quinces usually turn a lovely pink, though in my family extreme care was taken not to let that happen because a golden color was seen as superior and a sign of the cook's skill. Pink or golden, this jam tastes delicious on butter or cream-smeared barbarī bread with strong tea for breakfast. It's also delicious drizzled over rice pudding (page 218).

MAKES 1 PINT
(16 OZ) JAR
2 large quinces
3½ cups (1½ lb/700 g) sugar
1¾ cups (400 ml) water
3 tablespoons fresh lemon juice, plus more for squeezing

Peel and core the quinces and cut each quince into six wedges. Cut the wedges into thin slices and drop them into a bowl of water with a squeeze of lemon juice to prevent them from discoloring.

Put the sugar and water in a lidded pan over medium heat and bring to a gentle boil. Stir to dissolve the sugar. Drain the quince slices and add them to the pan. Bring back to a gentle boil, then reduce the heat to very low. Wrap a dish towel around the lid and tightly cover the pan. Simmer very gently for 2 hours, checking and stirring every 15 minutes. The quince will slowly absorb the syrup and the color will turn a deep red.

Remove the lid and increase the heat a little. Add the lemon juice and simmer until the syrup is as thick as runny honey. Test by dropping a little syrup on a plate chilled in the fridge for 10 minutes and drawing your fingertip through when it's cooled. If it wrinkles slightly the setting point has been reached. Pour the hot jam into a sterilized jar, allow to cool fully, put the lid on tightly, and store in the refrigerator. The syrup will thicken further after a day or two when the pectin in the quinces works its magic.

Morabbā-ye Pūst-e Līmū
Preserved Lemon Peel

You can use the following recipe with any citrus peel you have on hand, just bear in mind that with more bitter peel (such as Seville orange peel) you will need to repeat the boiling and rinsing to remove the bitterness. The peel can be cut in strips, squares or any shape you like. My mom cuts a very small circle from the top of sour oranges and empties the flesh with a spoon to keep the peel whole, which looks really pretty.

**MAKES 1 SMALL
(12 OZ) JAR**

3 lemons, oranges, or citrus fruit of your choice
1½ cups (10½ oz/300 g) sugar
1¼ cups (300 ml) water
Juice of 1 lemon

Cut the fruit in quarters and carefully remove the peel. With a sharp knife, slice away the membrane, but leave most of the white pith in place. Cut into slices.

Fill a medium-sized saucepan with cold water and add the peel. Bring to a boil and cook for 5 minutes. Drain well and rinse. Taste for bitterness and repeat this process as required. You may have to do this as many as four times.

Put the sugar and water in the saucepan and bring to a boil. Add the peel and cook over medium heat until the syrup thickens to the consistency of honey. Add the lemon juice and stir. Cook for a few minutes longer. Test for doneness by dropping a little of the syrup on a saucer chilled in the fridge for 10 minutes. Allow to cool and tap your finger on the surface of the syrup very gently. The syrup must stretch a little when you lift your finger. When the syrup has reached the desired thickness, pour the preserve into a sterilized jar, allow to cool fully before sealing, and store in the refrigerator.

Tea

Tea came to Iran from Russia in the eighteenth century and quickly became very popular. Our words for tea-making paraphernalia—samāvar, estekān—are Russian, as is our method of brewing tea in two stages. Serving tea is a ritual of hospitality. It is served as soon as guests arrive and several times afterwards.

Once tea cultivation began in the Caspian Sea area, particularly around Lahijan, tea became affordable for all and gradually replaced coffee, which had been drunk in Iran since the sixteenth century. Establishments where men gathered to drink coffee now served tea instead, but continued to be called ghahveh khāneh (coffee house).

Tea is sometimes flavored with a pinch of Earl Grey or a hint of cardamom, and is often taken with sugar cubes or rock candy (nabāt) and served with raisins, dried mulberries, and sweetmeats such as bāghlavā (page 42). We also enjoy a wide variety of herbal teas. A brew made with dried borage flowers and dried limes called chāy-e gol gāv zabān is probably our most popular and is drunk to boost health.

Here's how you can prepare tea at home, Persian style:

Black Tea: Bring water to a boil in a large stovetop kettle. Rinse a teapot that you can comfortably rest on top of your kettle or samovar. Put 1 teaspoon of loose-leaf black tea per person into the teapot and carefully add about 3½ tablespoons boiling water for every teaspoon of tea. Place the kettle back on the heat and remove the lid, then put the teapot on top of the kettle. Reduce the heat to very low so the water is only simmering. Allow the tea to brew for at least 10 minutes to release all the color and aroma from the tea leaves. Rinse tea glasses or cups with hot water and pour about 3½ tablespoons of the brewed tea into each one. Top up with boiling water and serve immediately.

Cardamom Tea: Add one very lightly crushed cardamom pod to the teapot with the dry tea.

Earl-Grey Scented Tea: Add a large pinch of Earl Grey tea for every teaspoon of regular black tea.

Cinnamon Tea: Add a small cinnamon stick to the teapot.

Chāy-e Gol Gāv Zabān: Rinse a teapot with boiling water and put 2 tablespoons dried borage flowers in the pot. Bash a dried lime with a rolling pin and add half of the lime to the pot with ½ cup (120 ml) water. Cover the pot with a tea cozy and allow to brew for 10 minutes. Strain into a cup and top up with boiling water from the kettle. Sweeten to taste with rock candy (nabāt) or sugar.

Coffee

Coffee is particuarly popular with Armenians and Iran's Arab population in the south-western province of Khuzestan. There may be bad blood between Armenians and Turks, historically speaking, but Armenians in Iran still call the thick coffee they so love ghahveh tork (Turkish coffee).

In Khuzestan, coffee is served with great ceremony and is called ghahveh arabī (Arabic coffee). The pot (daleh) used for making ghahveh arabī is similar to a tall teapot with a beak-like spout. Ghahveh arabī is taken without sugar but may be flavored with cardamom, cloves, saffron, or rosewater.

Reading coffee grounds to tell the future is a very a popular ritual both among Armenians and Khuzestani Arabs: once the coffee is drunk, the cup is inverted onto a saucer. The wet grounds create shapes and patterns which, once dried, can be read for one's fortune.

Ghahveh Tork: Put 1 tablespoon of Turkish coffee per person into a special Turkish coffee pot and add 1 teaspoon sugar and 1 full espresso cup of water per person and stir. Place the pot over low heat and gently bring to a boil. As soon as the foam on top starts rising, remove the pot from the heat and hold for a few seconds so the foam goes down. Repeat two more times. Divide the foam into espresso cups, then pour the coffee and serve immediately.

Ghahveh Arabī: Put 1 full espresso cup of water per person into a Turkish coffee pot and place over low heat. Once the water comes to a boil, remove from the heat for 30 seconds. Add 1 tablespoon of finely ground dark-roast coffee per person, stir, and return to the heat. Simmer very gently for about five minutes or until foam rises to the top. Remove from the heat and allow the foam to subside. Add a small pinch of cardamom and stir gently. Serve immediately in Turkish coffee cups or espresso cups.

Dūgh

Chilled Yogurt Drink

This simple healthy drink is often enjoyed with meals. A range of different herbs are used to flavor it—dried mint, pennyroyal, wild thyme: these herbs are considered "warm," while yogurt is a "cold" food (see page xv), and so the drink is balanced.

SERVES 1

Pinch of salt

Scant ½ cup (100 ml) plain yogurt

Pinch of dried mint, pennyroyal, or thyme

Still or sparkling water

Add a small pinch of salt to the yogurt and let it stand at room temperature for a day or two for it to slightly ferment.

Rub whatever dried herb you are using between your palms to pulverize it, add it to the yogurt, and beat with a whisk. Gradually add the water and continue whisking. Start with a ratio of half water to half yogurt and add more water if the drink is too thick. Add a few ice cubes and garnish with a sprig of mint.

Sharbat-e Tokhm-e Sharbatī
Rosewater and Wild Basil Seed Drink

Wild basil seeds are very similar to chia seeds, their distant relative, and swell when mixed with water in exactly the same way. Though chia seeds are larger, they make an excellent substitute. This refreshing drink is often sold by street vendors on hot days since it is thought to have a cooling effect on the body. Most Iranian households keep a small jar of wild basil seeds in stock so they can make this drink in summer or as a home remedy for coughs when the weather is cold.

SERVES 4

6 tablespoons wild basil or chia seeds

Generous ¾ cup (200 ml) water

1 cup (7 oz/200 g) sugar

1–2 tablespoons rosewater, as required

Ice

Fresh rose petals or mint leaves, to garnish

Put the wild basil or chia seeds in a sieve and rinse under running water. Place in a bowl and cover with tap water. Leave to stand for 30 minutes or more to swell. Pour off the excess water.

Heat the water and sugar in a small saucepan until the sugar dissolves to make a light simple syrup. Allow to cool a little, then chill in the fridge.

Add 1 tablespoon of the rosewater to the soaked seeds and divide among four tall glasses. Spoon a couple of tablespoons of the syrup into each glass and add some cold water. Taste, and top up with extra water or syrup to adjust the sweetness to your liking. You can use more rosewater too, if you wish. Add lots of ice. Garnish with fresh rose petals or mint leaves, and serve with stirrers or long spoons, since the seeds will keep sinking to the bottom.

Sharbat-e Sekanjabīn bā Khiyār

Caramel and Vinegar Cooler

The eleventh-century Persian polymath Avicenna prescribed sekanjabīn as a remedy for many common ailments. Called oxymel by the Romans, this vinegar and honey syrup has been highly regarded since ancient times for its medicinal properties. But sekanjabīn is not just medicine, it also makes a refreshing summer cooler. For non-medicinal pleasure, I use caramelised sugar instead of honey. The grated cucumber is optional, but a recommended addition.

SERVES 4

¾ cup (5 oz/150 g) sugar

2 cups (500 ml) boiling water

A few sprigs of mint

1 tablespoon white wine vinegar

½ English cucumber, grated or shredded

Ice cubes, to serve

Mint leaves, to garnish

Put the sugar in a small saucepan and place over medium-low heat without stirring. When the sugar turns a very light golden color, remove from the heat and carefully add the boiling water, then the mint and vinegar. Cover and leave to cool, then discard the mint.

Divide the grated cucumber among four tall glasses and pour 4–5 tablespoons of syrup into each glass. Add a few ice cubes and top up with cold water. Garnish with mint leaves and serve immediately.

Glossary

ĀB GHŪREH Verjuice is a tart juice extracted from unripe seedless grapes. It is used as a souring agent in stews and salad dressings. The fresh juice is either mixed with salt and boiled before bottling, or the bottled juice is left in the sun for a couple of weeks to develop a color similar to red wine vinegar.

ĀBGŪSHT Ābgūsht (also called dīzī) literally translates as "broth and meat" but can be much more than the sum of its parts. The basic version is a hotpot of lamb or chicken with legumes and potatoes. Like many rustic dishes, ābgūsht has many variations. Flavorings such as herbs, souring agents, and vegetables are often added. In Iran, a certain type of restaurant called dīzī-sara specializes in ābgūsht and the many condiments and side dishes that go with it. Dīzī refers to the individual stone or ceramic pots in which restaurants bake the hotpots. The broth is served separately, like a soup, with flatbread "croutons"—tīrīd/tīlīt or tīrīt in Farsi.

ADVIYEH This spice mix usually includes cinnamon, coriander, nutmeg, turmeric, cumin, black pepper, ground chili pepper, ginger, caraway, and cardamom, but the exact blend varies greatly from place to place. Mild curry powder is a good substitute, but the recipes in this book list the individual spices, since different brands vary hugely.

ĀLŪ BOKHĀRĀ A sweet and sour plum, blanched, skinned, and sun-dried for use in soups and stews. In some recipes, they can be replaced with dried apricots soured with a little lemon juice.

ANGELICA POWDER see golpar.

ĀRD-E NOKHOD Raw chickpea flour is mainly used in southern provinces to make Persian chive pakora, a spicy deep-fried street food of Indian origin. It is not suitable for baking or desserts. Raw chickpea flour is sold as besan or gram in South Asian grocery stores.

ĀRD-E NOKHODCHĪ Toasted, finely ground chickpea flour suitable for baking. It is used to make delicate cookies that melt in the mouth (nūn nokhodchī) and also to thicken the meat mixture for meatballs (kūfteh) and fritters (shāmī).

ĀSH Thick, stew-like soups. Most Persian soups are made with lots of greens and herbs. Legumes such as chickpeas, yellow lentils, green lentils, and dried beans are often included too. To thicken the soups, rice or ground rice, Persian soup noodles (reshte-ye āsh), and bulgur are used. Thinner soups are either of Western origin (called sūp) or of the eshkaneh type (see entry).

BABY GARLIC See sīr-e tāzeh.

BĀDEMJŪN There are two types of Persian eggplant—slender and long like Lebanese and some Asian eggplants, and smaller, fat eggplants similar to the Italian variety. Long eggplants are used in stews, while the chubby type is used for stuffing (dolmeh bādemjǔn). Small eggplants from Asian grocery stores work very nicely in stews. The thick eggplants sold in most supermarkets have a higher water content than Iranian eggplants, but can easily be substituted for both types used in Iran.

BĀGHĀLĪ Fresh fava beans are used in the rice dish bāghālī polō (page 34), but they also feature in some kūkū, kūfteh, and stews. Cooked fava beans in their pods are a favorite snack, often eaten with a pinch of golpar.

BARBARĪ An oval semi-flat bread with a chewy texture. It is usually sprinkled with sesame or nigella seeds. Barbarī is the bread of choice for breakfast, but is also served with many meals. See recipe on page 248.

BARBERRIES See zereshk.

BERENJ-E DŪDĪ Smoked rice is a highly prized ingredient from Iran that any gourmet must try at least once. It's made by smoking the sheaves of rice in small huts in Iran's rice-growing Caspian Sea area, and was originally a way of preserving rice.

BRINED UNRIPE GRAPES See ghūreh.

BŪRĀNĪ Būrānī or bōrānī refers to dishes of cooked vegetables mixed with yogurt. The most common are made with spinach (būrānī-ye esfenāj, page 255), zucchini (būrānī-ye kadū), eggplant (būrānī-ye bādemjūn, page 256), beets (būrānī-ye labū), and butternut squash (būrānī-ye kadū halvayī). In the province of Azarbaijan, būrānī often include a mix of vegetables and can be served as a main course.

CARAWAY See zīre-ye polōī.

CARDAMOM See hel.

CHĀSHNĪ Usually a souring agent used to flavor dishes. The most common are: lemon, lime, sour orange or pomegranate juice, verjuice, vinegar, pomegranate or plum molasses, tomato paste, or tamarind.

CHELŌ Plain steamed white rice. See recipe on page 236.

CHICKPEA FLOUR See ārd-e nokhod and ārd-e nokhodchī.

CORIANDER SEEDS See tokhm-e geshnīz.

CURRANTS See keshmesh polōi.

DATES See khormā.

DOLMEH Stuffed vegetables and leaves are popular throughout the Middle East and Western Asia. The leaves are stuffed with meat, rice, herbs, and yellow lentils and wrapped into parcels. Vegetables are hollowed out and then stuffed. Stuffed vine leaves (page 33), eggplants (page 144), cabbage leaves (pages 192), and quinces (page 138) are all very popular.

DRIED LIMES See līmū amānī.

ESHKANEH Refers to thin onion-based vegetarian soups flavored with herbs or fruits and eaten with flatbread "croutons." See recipes for eshkaneh-ye keshteh (with dried apricots, page 179) and eshkaneh-ye piyāz (with onions, page 181).

FAVA BEANS See bāghālī.

FENUGREEK GREENS See shambalīleh.

FLATBREAD See nān.

FRIED GARLIC See sīr dāgh.

FRIED MINT See na'nā dāgh.

FRIED ONIONS See piyāz dāgh.

GHALIYEH The ancient word for stew, as in ghaliyeh meygū (shrimp stew, page 184). See also khoresht.

GHEE see rōghan-e heyvānī.

GHŪREH These are grapes that are harvested before ripening, making them particularly tart. They lend their flavor to slow-cooked dishes such as khoresht-e bademjūn (page 76). If you are lucky enough to have a grape vine, freeze a few unripe grapes to use throughout the year. Ghūreh preserved in salty brine or verjuice for use in winter is called ghūreh ghūreh and can be found in Middle Eastern grocery stores.

GOLĀB Rosewater is much milder than rose essence, extract, or essential oil, but just a few drops is usually enough to flavor any dish. Never use strong rose essence, since it will completely overpower the dish.

GOL-E SORKH Dried Persian rose petals are available from Middle Eastern grocery stores and should be kept in a tightly covered jar in a cool, dry place. Perfumed roses are grown in Iran for their essence (which is used in rosewater) and for their petals, which are used in spice mixes. Rose petals also make a very tasty jam.

GOLPAR A spice obtained by grinding the seeds of heracleum persicum, a relative of the common hogweed. It is often sprinkled over pomegranate seeds and fava beans to add flavor and make them easier to digest. Golpar is often mistakenly labeled as Angelica powder. Angelica is a plant of the same family but Angelica powder comes from the root of the plant and cannot be used as a substitute.

HALVĀ Beside the famous tahini-based Middle Eastern halwā (halvā ardeh in Farsi), a number of other flour-based confections, flavored with saffron, cardamom, cinnamon, and rosewater, are called halvā in Iran. Halvā (flavored with saffron and rosewater), kuī halvā (halvā with butternut squash), halvā-ye gol (rose petal halvā, page 227), and halvā-ye havīj (carrot halvā) are some of the most popular.

HEL White and green cardamom is used to flavor many sweets, where it is often paired with rosewater. Cardamom is also a common component of the various Persian spice mixes. For sweet dishes, white cardamom and its seeds are preferred to green.

KABĀB Any grilled meat or vegetable is called kabāb in Farsi. Kabāb kūbīdeh (ground meat, page 70), kabāb barg (very thin slices of lamb tenderloin), and jūjeh kabāb (chicken or poussin, page 25) are popular. The word probably originally meant "cooked meat" as indicated by the names of ancient dishes such as tās kabāb (a layered meat and onion hotpot, page 191).

KALAM GHOMRĪ Kohlrabi, also known as kalam sang or ghonabīd in Farsi, is sweet and flavorful when sautéed or slowly steamed. It is used in stews, thick soups (āsh), and layered rice dishes such as kalam ghomrī polō (page 148).

KASHK This protein-rich ingredient is a by-product of churning butter from yogurt. The very low-fat yogurt that remains after the butter has been separated out is drained until quite thick. It is then shaped into small balls and dried. When required, the balls are soaked and ground to a thick paste. Ready-to-use kashk, a thick whitish liquid, and dry kashk are available from Middle Eastern grocery stores. It is usually quite salty and has a very distinctive flavor reminiscent of Norwegian brown cheeses (brunost), which are made from whey.

KATEH Plain rice made by the absorption method (see recipe on page 239). Kateh is preferred to chelō in the rice-growing province of Gilan.

KESHMESH POLŌI Currants and Zante currants are smaller and darker than raisins and have a sweet and sour flavor. They are used in many dishes, including rice with lentils (damī-ye adas or adas polō—see page 206). Chopped raisins can be substituted in most recipes.

KHELĀL-E BĀDŪM Slivered blanched almonds are used to garnish rice dishes, desserts, and other sweets, as well as featuring as the main ingredient in the elegant khoresht-e khelāl, page 129.

KHELĀL-E NĀRENJ The bitter peel of sour oranges (nārenj) is cut into fine slivers and sweetened by boiling in several changes of water to make jam. When boiled in a very light syrup, the slivers are used to make a very festive rice dish (shīrīn polō) or to garnish other dishes such as jeweled rice (morassa' polō, page 202). Seville orange peel is a very good substitute for sour orange peel.

KHELĀL-E PESTEH Slivered pistachios are made from a bright green variety and are used to garnish rice dishes, puddings, and sweets.

KHIYĀR SHŪR These crunchy miniature cucumbers are preserved in brine with tarragon, dill, garlic, and green chili peppers. Khiyār shūr is a staple of Persian sandwiches and wraps. See recipe on page 274.

KHORESHT Any stew eaten with rice is called khoresh or khoresht. In older Persian texts and some contemporary dialects, khoresht is known as ghaliyeh, as in ghaliyeh meygū (page 184).

KHORMĀ Dates. Iran is the world's second largest producer of dates; more than three hundred varieties are grown there. The two main types used in cooking are rotab-e mazāfati (a very moist black date) and khormā-ye zāhedi (a dry and almost blond variety). Dates are often steamed over rice, as in damī-ye adas (page 206) or used to make a thick sweet syrup (shīreh-ye khormā), vinegar, or aragh-e khormā, a strong alcoholic drink.

KOHLRABI See kalam ghomrī.

KOTLET These shallow-fried meat fritters are of Eastern European origin. While the Eastern European kotleti are usually made with pork and breadcrumbs, the Iranian version is made with beef or lamb and cooked or raw potatoes. Similar meat fritters with added ingredients such as yellow lentils, chickpeas, or herbs are called shāmī.

KŪFTEH Large meatballs made with ground lamb and rice or potatoes, and herbs, cooked in a savory or sweet and sour sauce. They are often stuffed with whole boiled eggs, currants, barberries, walnuts, and caramelized onions. There is a vegetarian version called yolchi kūftāsi (poor man's kūfteh) in Azarbaijan. Kūfteh means "pounded" in Persian.

KŪKŪ Crustless savory quiche-like dishes, usually served as a side dish. There are many different variations, including kūkū sībzamīnī tabrīzī (page 217) and kūkū sabzī (page 29).

LAPEH These yellow lentils are also known as split peas. For stews that call for lapeh, try to find the smallish Iranian ones or Indian chana dal. Chana dal cooks faster and can turn a little mushy, so if you are using them always parboil separately in salted water until cooked but with a firm bite in the center, and add to your stew or soup about ten minutes before serving.

LAVĀSH A paper-thin, tortilla-like bread baked in a clay oven. Lavāsh is sometimes air-dried to prolong storage. Dried lavāsh is then sprinkled with a little water a few minutes before use and wrapped in dish towels to soften. Hand-shaped lavāsh is available from most Middle Eastern grocers. Broken matzos or Italian carta di musica can be used instead to soak in the ābgūsht broth and in eshkaneh.

LĪMŪ AMĀNĪ Small Persian limes are boiled in salt water and then sun-dried. The fermentation process that takes place during drying imparts a smoky, musky flavor to the pulp and turns it a very dark brown. When cooked in a stew, the limes swell with the juices and release a delicious concentrated sour sauce when pressed with a fork.

MĀHI DŪDĪ In Iran's Caspian region smoked fish (usually kutum) is eaten in small amounts as a condiment. Whole smoked kutum is quite dry, salty, and golden in color. To prepare māhī dūdī, a piece is placed in a bowl over the rice as it steams. The steam softens the fish, which is then drained and flaked.

MALAS Refers to the sweet and sour, or to be exact sour and sweet, flavor of many dishes such as stuffed vegetables (dolmeh), meatballs (kūfteh), thick soups (āsh), and stews (khoresht). The flavor is created using sugar and a souring agent (chāshnī).

MARZEH Summer savory is a seasonal herb with a sharp, peppery flavor. It's often used to flavor the stuffing for vine leaves (page 33) and vegetables. Dried summer savory is a good substitute. Winter savory, not grown in Iran, tastes almost the same and is well worth growing in a sunny spot if you can.

MĀST-E CHEKĪDEH A very thick protein-rich dairy product, similar to Middle-Eastern labneh, often mixed with raw or cooked vegetables to make dips and side dishes. For the recipe see page 255.

MAZEH The word originally meant flavor or taste and was applied to a range of small dishes enjoyed with meals. Today it generally means small plates that accompany alcoholic drinks.

MŪSĪR A bulb in the onion family that grows wild in the Zagros mountains. It is mostly used in its dried form to flavor yogurt and pickles (torshī). Mūsīr is sometimes sold as Persian shallot or even spring garlic, but the flavor is very different from both. Sliced dried mūsīr must be refreshed in several changes of cold water before use to remove the bitterness, but mūsīr granules/powder can be used without soaking.

NABĀT Plain and saffron-flavored rock candy, which is used to sweeten tea and herbal infusions.

NĀN Flatbread. There are several different kinds of flatbread in Iran. Most of these have to be consumed on the day they are made. Each bakery usually makes only one variety, since the oven needed for each type is different. The most popular breads are lavāsh, sangak, barbarī (page 248), and tāftūn (page 246).

NA'NĀ DĀGH Dried mint heated in oil is used for garnishing and flavoring soups (āsh) and some other dishes, particularly to balance those considered to have a "cold" nature with the "heat" from mint. See recipe on page 276.

NĀRENJ Tart oranges, similar to Seville or marmalade oranges, have been grown in Iran since ancient times. The bitter peel is used in jams and rice dishes such as jeweled rice (page 202). The juice is used as a flavoring in soups, salads, and stews.

NIGELLA SEEDS See siyāh dūneh.

PANĪR Refers to all Persian cheeses, most of which are white and aged in brine, and many do not have specific names. The flavor of crumbly and salty white Cheshire cheese is remarkably similar to līqvān, a very popular sheep's cheese from eastern Azarbaijan. Greek feta, or any mild and creamy or crumbly sheep or goat cheese, are good substitutes.

PERSIAN BASIL See reyhān.

PERSIAN CUCUMBER PICKLES See khiyār shūr.

PERSIAN CUMIN See zīreh.

PERSIAN GOLDEN PLUMS See ālū bokhārā.

PERSIAN NOODLES FOR RICE See reshte-ye polōī.

PERSIAN SHALLOTS See mūsīr.

PERSIAN SOUP NOODLES See reshte-ye āsh.

PERSIAN SPICE MIX See adviyeh.

PESTEH Fresh pistachios appear in the markets around August. The kernels are encased in hard shells, as well as the soft skin that is used for making an aromatic preserve. Slivered pistachios (khelāl-e pesteh) are used to garnish rice dishes, stews, puddings, and other sweets.

PICKLED VEGETABLES See shūr and torshī.

PISTACHIOS See pesteh.

PIYĀZ DĀGH These fried onions add flavor to dishes and help thicken sauces for stews and soups. They are also used as a garnish. See recipe on page 276.

POLŌ This originally referred to parboiled rice layered with other ingredients such as vegetables and meat. Today it has come to mean any parboiled and steamed rice, whether plain or mixed with other ingredients.

POMEGRANATE MOLASSES See robb-e anār.

RESHTE-YE ĀSH Persian soup noodles are tossed in flour before drying, helping them to thicken soups. Linguini or udon noodles are good substitutes, but you may need to add a little flour to the broth. When using reshteh, only add salt at the last stage of cooking to avoid over-seasoning.

RESHTE-YE POLŌĪ These delicate brown noodles are added to special rice dishes such as reshteh polō (page 205). They are made from wheat flour and water and are toasted after drying. In some regional cuisines, they are boiled then steamed, as per the recipe for chelō (page 236) but, unlike rice, soaking beforehand is not required. Long vermicelli or angel hair pasta (capellini) can be used as a substitute after toasting in the oven (please see the recipe for reshteh polō).

REYHĀN There are several different varieties of Persian basil, all of which taste different from the Italian basil popular in the West, but Lemon basil and Thai basil work very well in most recipes. Basil is the herb of choice to accompany kabābs served with bread and is a key ingredient for sabzī khordan (page 98).

ROBB Any thick paste made from fruit or vegetables for flavoring food is called robb. The most common is rob-be gōjeh farangī (tomato), now often simply referred to as robb, but there is also rob-be anār (pomegranate), rob-be sīb-e torsh (apple), rob-be ālūcheh (mirabelles), and rob-be azgīl (medlar).

ROBB-E ANĀR This pomegranate paste is traditionally made by reducing the juice of sour, or sweet and sour, pomegranates until very thick and dark. The paste is sold by weight in markets and can vary hugely in sourness. Bottled robb-e anār is thinner and sweeter and is often sold as pomegranate molasses or syrup.

ROCK CANDY See nabāt.

RŌGHAN-E HEYVĀNĪ Persian ghee has a slightly different flavor from the Indian version. In Iran, milk is first turned into yogurt, then the yogurt is fermented and churned for butter. The fermented yogurt particles remaining in the ghee caramelize during cooking and give it a lovely nutty flavor. Melted or clarified butter, or Indian ghee are all good substitutes.

ROSE PETALS See gol-e sorkh.

ROSEWATER See golāb.

SAFFRON Bright red saffron comes from the saffron crocus flower. The stigmas have to be handpicked then dried. Saffron is usually used in the form of saffron water (see page 278). The red color changes to a deep yellow once added to other ingredients.

SANGAK A long wholewheat bread baked on a bed of hot pebbles on the floor of an oven similar to, but much larger than, a pizza oven. It doesn't keep well, but can be frozen and toasted when needed.

SAR GONJESHKĪ These versatile little meatballs, also known as kalleh gonjeshkī, kūfteh ghelgheli, and kūfteh rīzeh, are used in soups, rice dishes, and stews. See recipe on page 282.

SHĀHĪ The oval leaves of the Persian cress plant are mildly peppery. The name of the plant in Persian translates to "royal herb." Shāhī is one of several herbs used in sabzī khordan (page 98). Like cress, shāhī will grow very fast from seeds.

SHAMBALĪLEH Fenugreek leaves are a little bitter, but impart a unique flavor and aroma to dishes such as ghormeh sabzī (page 79). Fresh and dried fenugreek can be found in most South Asian grocery stores and some supermarkets, where it is usually called methi. Fenugreek seeds are used as a spice and cannot be substituted for the greens.

SHĀMĪ These meat fritters originated in the Levant, which used to be called Shām before Syria and Lebanon became independent. Similar in appearance to falafel, they are made with lamb or beef and boiled yellow lentils. See recipe on page 22.

SHŪR These brined vegetable pickles are a wonderful accompaniment to many dishes and are delicious in sandwiches. A medley of vegetables is flavored with lots of dill, cilantro, tarragon, garlic, and hot chili peppers. See recipe on page 273.

SĪR DĀGH Fried garlic is used for garnishing and flavoring thick soups (āsh) and other dishes such as kashk-e bādemjūn (see page 212).

SĪR-E TĀZEH One of the harbingers of spring, baby garlic is sold in huge bunches around the Iranian new year (Nōrūz). It is very mild and looks like baby leeks. Both the white bulb and the green leaves are edible. The bulb is often eaten raw and the long green leaves are used to flavor dishes including sabzī polō (page 13) and kūkū sabzī (page 29). If you feel like growing your own, just tuck a few fat garlic cloves into the ground or in a pot, after the first frosts or in spring. The bulbs will continue growing leaves after each harvest and you will have a steady supply if you leave the white bulb undisturbed.

SIYĀH DŪNEH Nigella seeds, also known as black onion seeds or kalonji, have a slightly bitter herby flavor. They are used to garnish and flavor flatbreads and pickles (torshī).

SLIVERED ALMONDS See khelāl-e bādūm.

SLIVERED PISTACHIOS See khelāl-e pesteh.

SMOKED FISH See māhī dūdī.

SMOKED RICE See berenj-e dūdī.

SOMĀGH Sumac is a reddish brown powder obtained from the berries of the sumac bush. It is used for its lemony flavor and is usually sprinkled over kabābs and rice.

SOUR GRAPES See ghūreh.

SOUR ORANGE See nārenj.

SOUR ORANGE PEEL See khelāl-e nārenj

STRAINED Yogurt See māst-e chekīdeh.

SUMAC See somāgh.

SUMMER SAVORY See marzeh.

SŪP In Farsi, the word sūp refers only to brothy Western-style soups. The most popular of these are chicken and noodle soup (sūp-e morgh), barley soup (sūp-e jō), and mushroom soup (sūp-e ghārch).

TĀFTŪN One of the oldest breads baked in Iran, tāftūn is similar to Indian naan, though thinner and lighter in texture. Traditionally baked in small clay ovens, tāftūn is round and large with lots of big bubbles on its surface.

TAHCHĪN A savory rice dish with a thick golden crust, tahchīn is made from a mixture of parboiled rice, egg, saffron, and yogurt, topped with lamb or chicken and then covered with another layer of rice in the form of a cake. It is then steamed slowly to allow a crust to form. See the recipe for tahchīn-e esfenaj (page 152).

TAHDĪG This is the crispy layer that forms in the bottom of a pot of steamed rice—the word literally means "bottom of the pot." For tahdīg options, see page 230.

TAMARIND See tamr-e hendī.

TAMR-E HENDĪ Tamarind is a tart podded fruit with bean-like seeds. The fermented pods make a brown paste that is used as a souring agent in many cuisines. In Iran, tamarind is sold as a pulp, which is soaked and sieved before use. Tamarind paste, available internationally, doesn't require soaking or sieving. Different brands vary hugely in acidity so add small amounts and taste as you go to get the right balance.

TAREH Persian chives are closely related to leeks. They have thin flat leaves and a rather sharp flavor with a hint of garlic. In some recipes it is possible to substitute chives or the delicate green leaves from leeks. Chinese chives and Middle Eastern kurrat are related and have a similar flavor, and kale can be substituted in some recipes, too.

TARKHŪN Tarragon is an aniseed-flavored herb and one of the ingredients of sabzī khordan (page 98). There are two types of tarragon, French and Russian. The tarragon used in Iranian dishes is the pungent French variety.

TARRAGON See tarkhūn.

TĀS KABĀB A number of layered, slow-cooked lamb and vegetable hotpots are called tās kabāb—"kabāb made in a pot." The traditional tās kabāb is made with lamb, onions, and potatoes, but tās kabāb-e bādemjūn (lamb and eggplant) and tās kabāb-e beh (lamb and quince, page 191) are also popular. Making all of these with chicken instead of lamb has become increasingly popular.

TOKHM-E GESHNĪZ Coriander seeds, sold both whole and ground, have a very sweet smell and are used to flavor many dishes, pickles, and even sweets.

TOKHM-E SHARBATĪ These wild basil seeds are used to make a refreshing summer drink (see page 299). The seeds swell and form a gel when soaked, taking on a lovely blue-grey color. Chia seeds are larger but a very good substitute.

TORSHĪ No meal is complete without a bowl of these pickles, of which there are a multitude of varieties. Many are fiery hot and very tart. An array of vegetables are used as well as herbs and fruits. They usually require a month or so to develop the flavor, but some can be eaten after a day or two.

TINY MEATBALLS See sar gongeshkī.

VERJUICE See āb ghūreh.

WILD BASIL SEEDS See tokhm-e sharbatī.

YELLOW LENTILS See lapeh.

ZERESHK Dried barberries are an important ingredient in Persian cooking. They are mainly used in rice dishes, but are also a favorite garnish to lend a bit of color and tartness. Store them in an airtight jar, or a ziplock bag in the freezer or fridge.

ZĪREH Also known as Persian cumin or caraway, these aromatic seeds are related to cumin but are much smaller and darker. Zīreh features in most Persian spice mixes and is widely used, whole or ground, to flavor breads, pickles (torshī), soups, and stews. Regular cumin can be used instead.

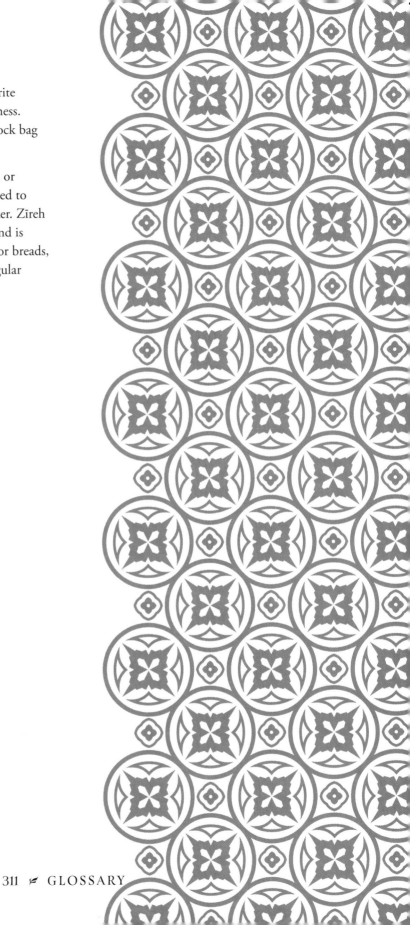

Index

Acknowledgments

I don't even know where to begin! This book wouldn't have been possible without all the beautiful people in my life who inspired me, ate my food, listened to my stories, encouraged me to write, and helped me out. So many people have given me support and advice to get this book in order, it would be hard to name all so I'm going to keep this short and simple.

First and foremost, I'd like to thank my agent Andrew Lownie for trusting me and for his invaluable advice.

Thank you to my family and friends for encouragement and inspiration. Hossein, thank you for supporting me through the years in every possible way. Souren, my lovely son, thank you for your "constructive criticism" and encouragement and thanks for putting up with me when all I could think of was my work. Hossein, Lubna, Patricia, and Arash, thank you for helping me out with finding the right equipment for my photography and the props for my photos and styling. I know I was sometimes annoyingly hard to please and dragged you from place to place in search of things like the perfect pomegranate for a picture. I simply can't thank you enough.

A big thank you to my editor Madeleine O'Shea, designer Jessie Price, and the rest of the team at Head of Zeus for their hard work. And thank you to Jessica Griffiths for the lovely cover photo.

And last but not least, dear Nigel Slater, thank you. You may not even remember but your advice set me on the right track. I'll never forget your kindness and encouragement.

AZERBAIJAN

AZERBAIJAN
ARMENIA
AZERBAIJAN

TURKEY

Khvoy

Marand
Tabrīz
Āzarbāyjān-e Sharqī
Ardabīl
Ardabīl

Qezel Su
Caspian

Orūmīyeh
Marāgheh
Qaranqu
Miāndoāb
Āzarbāyjān-e Gharbī
Mahābād
Būkān
Saqqez
Tatāu
Qezel Ozan
Qezel Ozan
Zanjān
Zanjān
Sefīd

Bandar-e Anzalī

Rasht
Gīlān

Qazvīn
Qazvīn

Nazarābād
Shahrīyār

SYRIA

Kordestān

Sanandaj
Hamadān

Hamadān

Markazī
Sāveh

Qom

Kermānshāh
Kermānshāh

Malāyer
Malāyer
Arāk

Borūjerd

Lorestān

Īlām
Khorramābād
Do Rūd

Īlām
Samreh

IRAQ

Dez

Andīmeshk
Dezfūl
Kho
Shahr
Kord

JORDAN

Shūshtar
Khūzestān
Masjed-e
Soleymān
Īzeh

Karūn
Chahā
va B

Ahvāz

Kohgīlū
Bowyer

Al Başrah
Khorramshahr
Ābādān

Bandar-e
Māhshahr

Jarāh

Damāgheh-ye
Bahrgān

Ra's osh Sha
Band
Būsh

KUWAIT

The

SAUDI

ARABIA

© Global Mapping Ltd

B